D0932846

Photograph by Arnold Genthe

S. S. MC CLURE

THE AUTOBIOGRAPHY OF S. S. McCLURE

WILLA CATHER

Introduction to the Bison Books Edition by
ROBERT THACKER

University of Nebraska Press
Lincoln and London

Introduction © 1997 by the University of Nebraska Press
Manufactured in the United States of America

☉ The paper in this book meets the minimum require-
ments of American National Standard for Information
Sciences—Permanence of Paper for Printed Library
Materials, ANSI Z39.48-1984.

First Bison Books printing: 1997
Most recent printing indicated by the last digit below:
10   9   8   7   6   5   4   3   2   1

Library of Congress Cataloging-in-Publication Data
Cather, Willa, 1873–1947.
The autobiography of S. S. McClure / Willa Cather;
introduction to the Bison Books edition by Robert
Thacker.
p. cm.
"Originally published as My autobiography by S. S.
McClure in 1914 by Frederick A. Stokes, New York"—T.p.
verso.
ISBN 0-8032-6373-2 (pbk.)
1. McClure, S. S. (Samuel Sidney), 1857–1949.   2.
McClure's magazine.   I. McClure, S. S. (Samuel Sidney),
1857–1949. My autobiography.   II. Title.
PN4874.M35C38   1997
070.4'1'092—dc20
[B]
96-43609   CIP

Originally published as *My Autobiography* by S. S.
McClure in 1914 by Frederick A. Stokes, New York.
Reprinted from the original.

INTRODUCTION

Robert Thacker

Willa Cather's personal copy of this book bears the following inscription:

> With affectionate regard
> for the real author
> S. S. McClure
> New York City Dec. 14 1914

Unlike the more equivocal headnotes that accompanied the publication of his autobiography, first in *McClure's* from October 1913 through May 1914 and then in the book versions published in New York by Frederick A. Stokes and in Britain by John Murray in late 1914, McClure's inscription here confirms that Cather is this book's author.[1] And unlike her relation to *The Life of Mary Baker Eddy* (1909), Cather never disputed her role in McClure's book; rather, just as the final installment had appeared in *McClure's* she was writing to Will Owen Jones, her former mentor in Lincoln, that she had enjoyed writing the biography because McClure was so honest about it and was not for dressing up the truth any. He told her the facts just as he remembered them, she wrote, and he wanted them put down that way.[2]

As Cather's critical stature has grown in recent years, much has been made of the time she spent working on *McClure's* from 1906 through 1912, especially on the various contacts and experiences it occasioned: the brief but crucial friendship with Sarah Orne Jewett, the travel abroad, the rise to the prominent magazine's

managing editorship. Cather's subsequent drive to
break free of the magazine for time to write her novels
has garnered further comment.[3] To some degree, this
progression was a matter of Cather's breaking free of
S. S. McClure himself. Indeed, Hermione Lee has gone
so far as to pronounce the writing of McClure's autobiography Cather's "last piece of subservient hack work."[4]
Perhaps, if seen a particular way, but the relation between Willa Cather and S. S. McClure—each a major
presence in American letters during the first decades
of this century—is a complex one, even a symbiotic one
during Cather's years on *McClure's*.

While living in Pittsburgh, Cather had unsuccess-
fully submitted stories to *McClure's*, but she did not
come to its editor's attention until she was recom-
mended to H. H. McClure, his cousin, by Will Owen
Jones in Lincoln. Keeping an eye out for emerging
writers and potential staff members for the magazine
was one of S. S. McClure's key editorial precepts, so he
summoned her to New York City in May 1903. As a
letter she wrote to Jones a few days after their meeting shows quite emphatically, Cather was transformed
by him: McClure so impressed her by his enthusiasm,
by his deep interest in her, and especially by his attitude toward her writing that she almost instantly became, according to James Woodress, "his captive for life."
Convinced that he had a find in Cather, McClure for
his part decided at once to foster this Pittsburgh
schoolteacher's writing ambitions: he would publish all
her stories in his magazine from then on or place them
elsewhere; his publishing house would bring out a book
of Cather's stories after first using them in *McClure's*;
he even called his employees who had rejected Cather's
stories into the office and, in her presence, demanded
that they account for themselves.[5]

As founder and editor of one of the leading magazines in the country, the man who had made "muck-
raking" synonymous with the era, S. S. McClure could
do all these things for Cather, and he did. And three
years later, in 1906, when he was confronted with the
mass resignations of the principal staff members who
had made his magazine famous—Ray Stannard Baker,
John S. Phillips, Lincoln Steffens, Ida M. Tarbell and
others—McClure swooped into Pittsburgh and convinced Cather to come work for him. She did—for the
whole trajectory of her life had been leading her east
from Red Cloud to the center of things, New York City—
so what McClure was offering was her main chance.
Yet as she joined its staff in the spring of 1906,
McClure's was, despite all appearances, a sinking ship—
from that year on the magazine never made a profit
despite circulation of more than 400,000 copies. S. S.
McClure had so extended his company that its financial collapse was inevitable while she was there. And
with that collapse—which came in 1912 through a financial reorganization that forced him out—came both
McClure's personal demise and Cather's escape from
magazine work. When he died in 1949, two years after
Cather, McClure's obituary noted that he had been "virtually retired since 1914," the year his autobiography
completed serialization and appeared as a book.[6]
Financial matters to one side, McClure for a time
kept at what he was most about after Cather's arrival
in New York: publishing a magazine as imaginatively
various as could be made. The key to his formula was
his policy of sending writers off to take as much time
as needed to obtain excellence. Once she had gathered
the Mary Baker Eddy material, which the magazine
published during 1907–8, Cather's position at *McClure's*
was assured. Though she became managing editor,

Ellery Sedgwick wrote that Cather, "secure in her respected genius, remained apparently unmindful of office thunderstorms." The energetic and imaginative McClure was a hard man to work for. But during the years of Cather's association with him, they developed a harmonious and mutually respectful relationship, one they sustained despite infrequent contact throughout the rest of their lives. As Woodress writes, "Next to her father and brothers he was the most important man in her life. Her devotion to McClure, however, was a hindrance to her career, for he kept her editing his magazine long after she should have been channeling all her creative energies into writing fiction." McClure, for his part, responded in kind. As Edith Lewis, Cather's coworker at *McClure's* and longtime companion, later wrote, McClure "not only had great respect for Willa Cather's judgment; he believed absolutely in her integrity, which among the vanities and jealousies and ambitions that so often surrounded him was, I think, a sort of oasis for his restless spirit. And I think also that he found in her something which heightened his pleasure in his magazine—which gave him back his old youthful excitement and pride in being an editor, and made him feel that the game was worth while."[7]

Most scholars see Cather's trip to the Southwest during the spring of 1912 as the turning point in her career. Woodress, for example, uses her departure then as a prologue for his biography—the moment at which she sees both the aesthetic path before her in what becomes *O Pioneers!* (1913) and breaks away from the magazine. And while she was away, Cather heard from McClure about both his proposed autobiography and his business troubles. A letter she wrote from Winslow, Arizona, in April begins with an eager offer to help with the autobiography while another, written from

Red Cloud, after she had begun her return east, more
practically considers various problems—writing to suit
McClure, writing in another person's voice, wondering
where to do the work—but never wavering in her expressions of willingness, gratitude, and sympathy for
McClure's predicament.[8]
     For McClure and Cather, each, the writing of the
autobiography was a signal act. For him, it was a chance
to formalize a version of himself he had been present-
ing orally to audiences for some time and, even more
directly, a way of reasserting his presence and partici-
pation in the world's affairs just as he was effectively
done with the magazine he had founded in 1893.[9] He
had to find another career. For her, it was a task not of
"hack work" but rather one which allowed her to look
both backward and forward—back, out of gratitude for
all that McClure had done for her by bringing her to
New York, encouraging her, and publishing her work.
But written as it was during the summer of 1913 just
after she had completed *O Pioneers!*, Cather's work on
the autobiography advanced her movement toward the
writing that would make her famous. It allowed her to
experiment with voice, form, and the presentation of a
particular construction of character. As she indicates
in the same 1914 letter to Will Owen Jones, Cather
went from McClure's life to her own in *The Song of the
Lark* (1915), her "most thinly veiled autobiography," according to Susan J. Rosowski, and after that, moved on
to her novel that most directly displays the effects of
McClure's autobiography, *My Ántonia*—Cather's title
echoing McClure's, *My Autobiography*. Cather confided
to Jones that she felt competent to manage a male point
of view in *My Ántonia* because of her severe training
in writing McClure's book.[10]
     That training was later described in detail—presum-

ably with Cather's approval—by her longtime secretary, Sarah J. Bloom, in a 1944 letter to Edward Wagenknecht:

> As you have said, Miss Cather did write Mr. McClure's autobiography. The method she pursued was rather interesting. Once a week Mr. McClure came to Miss Cather's apartment, sat down, said, "Now, where did I stop last time?" and then resumed his story where he had left off the week before. He was perfectly at ease with Miss Cather because she had worked with him for several years as managing editor of his magazine. He simply remembered out loud. Miss Cather doesn't know shorthand. The next day she began writing it out in longhand. Then I used to copy it for her on the typewriter. She said it was very good practice in writing 'conversation' exactly as she had heard it. All of Mr. McClure's characteristic phrases staid in her mind.[11]

McClure had been on the lecture circuit for the several years previous to the autobiography—indeed, such occasions were to be an important source of income for him once he was out of the magazine. So McClure was well-practiced at telling his version of his own history; literally, he embodied the Horatio Alger myth and he presented himself as such, both to his audiences and—judging from the text here—to Cather during their sessions.

Writing in *Willa Cather* (1953), the first biography of the author, E. K. Brown observed that "Technically *My Autobiography* . . . belongs to the canon of Willa Cather's writings, but she was right in her opinion that in every sense that matters it was McClure's." Brown's view has held sway since. Cather scholars have paid scant attention to the book; it has been of more interest to historians looking at the Progressive era and muckraking. McClure's biographer, Peter Lyon, wrote of *My Autobiography* that "what was effective as a series of magazine articles added up to trivial autobiography" and Ellen Moers, introducing Lyon's book in a new edition, calls the autobiography "a dull and proper document with none of its subject's flamboyance showing. . . ."[12]

Such assessments fail to recognize major considerations, however, that warrant the reprinting of this book as a part of the Cather canon. Most important are the timing of this project in Cather's own development—suggested above—and her success at recreating McClure's persona. Indeed, his wife and his closest associates—many of whom had known him from youth—thought she had captured his characteristic ways of speaking.[13] More pointedly, the book's contemporary reception was one which wholly rejected the negative view advanced by Lyon and Moers. First, *My Autobiography* struck a chord as a serial—McClure received scores of effusive letters as it ran in *McClure's*, both from the famous (W. D. Howells, Booth Tarkington, and Josephus Daniels, the Secretary of the Navy) as well as from the obscure. In fact, the magazine was able to extend the serial into June by publishing a selection of the letters McClure had received. As a book, it was praised without exception. Elia W. Peattie in the *Chicago Tribune* described it as "a story so typically American, so guiltless of literary pose, so vigorous and simple in the telling that in reading it one is transported beyond the room in which he sits and the page he peruses, and sees young Sam McClure's life, with its bitter hardships, its keen adventures, and its valorous little triumphs as if it were a living thing enacted before the eyes." Its "first half," she wrote, "is classic in its directness, its simplicity, its complete actuality." The *Denver News* maintained that McClure "has—and unconsciously, too—avoided every fault that usually characterizes the self-told story of the self-made man." In the *Springfield (Mass.) Union*, the reviewer protested that it "is a book difficult to review. It is a book that one reads without a thought of its literary quality. Something in it is the biography of each of its readers." Striking a similar note—as did virtually all the contemporary reviewers—the *Washington Star* notice concluded that "The whole is as clean-cut, as simple, as symmetrical, as classic as an elm tree. And it is all the time human." British reviewers were equally positive. The *London Standard* called it "a most ingratiating book," and *The Spectator* saw it as "a plain and unvarnished record of a life of ceaseless effort."[14]

What these reviewers found in *The Autobiography of S. S. McClure*, by Willa Cather, was the very simplicity, the very unadorned directness, the complex, unstated, unaffected empathy that was about to become its author's hallmark as a writer of fiction. This would be seen most especially in *The Song of the Lark* and *My Ántonia,* but it is also apparent in such books as *A Lost Lady* (1923) and *The Professor's House* (1925). More immediately, McClure and his autobiography contributed to Cather's short fiction. In "Ardessa" (1917), the editor O'Malley, patterned on McClure, is publisher of a *McClure's*-like magazine called *The Outcry*. But in another story written while she was working on *My Ántonia,* "Her Boss" (1919), Cather draws directly on her experience in composing McClure's autobiography and anticipates much of her future fiction. She has Paul Wanning, a successful lawyer dying of a kidney ailment, dictate his own autobiography to one of the firm's young secretaries, whom he has singled out for her human—as opposed to her "businesslike"—qualities:

> But walking up and down his private office, with the strong afternoon sun pouring in at his windows, a fresh air stirring, all the people and boats moving restlessly down there, he could say things he wanted to say. It was like living his life over again.
>
> He did not miss his wife or his daughters. He had become again the mild, contemplative youth he was in college, before he had a profession and a family to grind for, before the two needs which shape our destiny had made him pretty much what they make of every man.[15]

S. S. McClure, famous New York publisher, is in this passage, just as the young woman was who met him in 1903 and was immediately enraptured by him, ready to go to the stake for him.[16] In telling his story to Cather he was "living his life over," becoming again a small boy in Ireland, and then a bit larger boy in Indiana, a student at college in Illinois, a young man in love trying to woo his beloved and make his way, an accomplished man of business and affairs, shaking up the world—still the boy he had been, yet somehow was no longer, detached from his previous being. And as she listened to McClure tell this story, Willa Cather made it her own and made it, too, part of the stories of the numerous characters who were to spring from her fecund imagination.

As she listened to McClure, Cather was ruminating over her own story. Her experience with McClure would go into creating Thea Kronborg, and then Jim Burden—who also worked in a New York law firm—and eventually Godfrey St. Peter—who also "did not miss his wife or his daughters" and became again the young person he had been, as did Burden, and Thea too. S. S. McClure, dictating his story, is present in all these fictions. And like the story she shaped for McClure here, Cather's own last story, "The Best Years" (1948), takes readers back to her own girlhood in Red Cloud; it is the last stop on her fictional "road home." Though well embarked on that road by the time she came to write *The Autobiography of S. S. McClure*, in that intimate task—the writing of the life story of a man she knew so well, as she told Jones—Willa Cather found the forms that led her from *My Autobiography* to *My Ántonia* and then to the later fiction that has confirmed Cather as an American writer of the very first rank.[17]

NOTES

1. I am grateful to Dr. Robert and Mrs. Doris Kurth, the present owners of Cather's copy, for providing me with a photocopy of McClure's inscription.

The *McClure's* serialization began with this headnote: "I wish to express my indebtedness to Miss Willa Sibert Cather for her invaluable assistance in the preparations of these memoirs." See *McClure's* (October 1913): 33. This was subsequently changed to the note appearing here (xxv). In the same vein, McClure wrote to a friend that "Miss Cather is due the largest part of the literary success. She is profoundly responsible for this book. It is of course written exactly as I wanted it. I take great credit for the work from the standpoint of an editor but to her I must give most of the credit from the standpoint of a writer." S. S. McClure to Mrs. Cale Young Rice, 6 April 1914, Lilly Library, Indiana University.

2. See Willa Cather and Georgine Milmine, *The Life of Mary Baker G. Eddy and the History of Christian Science*, (New York: Doubleday, Page, 1909; rpt. with introduction and afterword David Stouck, Lincoln: University of Ne-

braska Press, 1993). Willa Cather to Will Owen Jones, 29 May 1914, Clifton Waller Barrett Library, University of Virginia.

3. See, for example, Sharon O'Brien, *Willa Cather: The Emerging Voice* (New York: Oxford University Press, 1987).

4. Hermione Lee, *Willa Cather: Double Lives* (New York: Pantheon, 1989), 82.

5. Willa Cather to Will Owen Jones, 7 May 1903, Clifton Waller Barrett Library, University of Virginia. James Woodress, *Willa Cather: A Literary Life* (Lincoln: University of Nebraska Press, 1987), 171.

6. "S. S. M'Clure Dead; Publisher Was 92," *The New York Times,* 23 March 1949, 27. For McClure's life, and especially a detailing of his demise, see Peter Lyon, *Success Story: The Life and Times of S. S. McClure* (New York: Scribner's, 1963), 210–337 and *passim.*

7. Ellery Sedgwick, *The Happy Profession* (Boston: Little, Brown, 1946), 145. Cather's ongoing devotion to McClure is seen, most notably, in a public embrace she spontaneously gave him on stage when each of them received an award from the National Institute of Arts and Letters in 1944. See Woodress, *A Literary Life*, 498. See also Willa Cather to S. S. McClure, 26 May [1933?], and Willa Cather to S. S. McClure, 26 May 1944, Lilly Library, Indiana University; Willa Cather to Mrs. Marie Adelaide Belloc Lowndes, 4 October 1944, Harry Ransom Humanities Research Center, University of Texas. Woodress, 171–72. There Woodress also notes that in later years Cather contributed to McClure's support when he was largely without means. Edith Lewis, *Willa Cather Living: A Personal Record* (New York: Alfred A. Knopf, 1953), 71.

8. Willa Cather to S. S. McClure, 22 April [1912], 9 and 12 June [1912], Lilly Library, Indiana University.

9. See Robert Stinson, "S. S. McClure's *My Autobiography*: The Progressive as Self-Made Man," *American Quarterly*, 22 (1970): 203–12. Stinson cites a detailed account of one of McClure's lectures from the *Springfield (Mass.) Republican* (31 January 1910) in the McClure papers at Indi-

ana to maintain that "McClure had been telling people about his past for years by 1913, and though Willa Cather actually wrote *My Autobiography*, there is far more in it of McClure than of Willa Cather" (206).

10. Susan J. Rosowski, "Willa Cather and the Intimacy of Art, Or: In Defense of Privacy," *Willa Cather Pioneer Memorial Newsletter*, 36 (1992–93), 50. Willa Cather to Will Owen Jones, 20 May 1919, Clifton Waller Barrett Library, University of Virginia.

11. Sarah J. Bloom to Edward Wagenknecht, 20 October 1944, Pierpont Morgan Library, New York City.

12. E. K. Brown, *Willa Cather: A Critical Biography*, completed by Leon Edel (New York: Alfred Knopf, 1953; rpt. Lincoln: University of Nebraska Press, 1987), 182. Lyon, *Success Story*, 347. Ellen Moers, Introduction, *Success Story* by Peter Lyon (Deland, Florida: Everett/Edwards, 1967), x. McClure's letter to Mrs. Cale Young Rice, cited above, contains a relevant sentence: "Of course you and I realize more than other people how mild this autobiography is compared to the material."

13. John S. Phillips, one of McClure's classmates at Knox College and among those who left *McClure's* just before Cather's arrival, wrote, "It is a wonderfully fine piece of work that you are doing in that autobiography. It is so humanly interesting, and written with truth and simplicity. I suppose you owe something to Miss Cather, but it seems you just the same." John S. Phillips to S. S. McClure, 19 March 1914, Lilly Library, Indiana University. Willa Cather to Mrs. S. S. McClure, 10 December 1913, Lilly Library, Indiana University. Cather recalls these reactions to the autobiography in her May 1919 letter to Will Owen Jones.

14. Elia W. Peattie, "Mr. McClure Tells All about Himself," *Chicago Tribune,* 19 September 1914; "The Life Story of a Genius," *Denver News,* 27 September 1914; "Autobiography New Gospel for the Ambitious," *Springfield (Mass.) Union,* 20 September 1914; Rev. of *My Autobiography, Washington Star,* 19 September 1914; "A Fighter Against Odds," *London Standard,* 7 December 1914; "Mr. McClure's Auto-

biography," *The Spectator,* 21 November 1914, 717–18. These reviews, and numerous others offering the same sentiments, are contained in a clipping file in the McClure Papers, Lilly Library, Indiana University.

15. Willa Sibert Cather, "Her Boss," *Smart Set* (October 1919): 104. Willa Sibert Cather, "Ardessa," *The Century* (May 1918): 105–16. These are reprinted in *Uncle Valentine and Other Stories: Cather's Uncollected Short Fiction, 1915–1929,* edited by Bernice Slote (Lincoln: University of Nebraska Press, 1973).

16. Willa Cather to Will Owen Jones, 7 May 1903, Clifton Waller Barrett Library, University of Virginia.

17. Ironically, the title used here, *The Autobiography of S. S. McClure* was the title that appeared on McClure's contract with his New York publisher, Frederick A. Stokes. It is in the McClure Papers, Lilly Library, University of Indiana.

CONTENTS

CHAPTER I

CHAPTER II

CHAPTER III

CHAPTER IV

CHAPTER V

CHAPTER VI

CONTENTS

ILLUSTRATIONS

xxiii

I T WILL be seen from this narrative that to my mother and to my wife I owe much. I am indebted to the coöperation of Miss Willa Sibert Cather for the very existence of this book.

Throughout my life I have had the good fortune to experience kindliness, consideration and helpfulness from many people. Among those whom I remember with especial affection was the late Mr. William M. Laffan, of the New York Sun, a man singularly loyal and generous. I owe much to Melville B. Anderson (formerly Professor of English Literature at Knox College, now Professor Emeritus of Leland Stanford), who first encouraged me to hope that I might find a place in the world. I was fortunate in my three employers: Col. A. A. Pope, Roswell Smith, and Theodore L. De Vinne. I have told something of these three men in the following pages, but have scarcely expressed my appreciation of their high ability. I wish here to emphasize my indebtedness to the consideration and assistance of my long-time associates, Miss Ida M. Tarbell and Mr. John S. Phillips.

I have said in this book very little of the last
fifteen years of my life. Much of that time has been
spent abroad, in travel and investigation in many
countries. The most important results of these
years I have tried to state briefly in the last
chapter.   S. S. McCLURE.

THE AUTOBIOGRAPHY OF S. S. McCLURE

CHAPTER I

MY EARLY CHILDHOOD—THE ROAD TO BALLY-
MONEY—PEAT CUTTING—MY EARLY SCHOOL-
ING—MY FATHER DIES—WE SAIL FOR
AMERICA

I WAS born in Ireland, fifty-six years ago.
Antrim, the northeast county of the Province
of Ulster, was my native county. My mother's
maiden name was Elizabeth Gaston. Her people
were descended from a French Huguenot family
that came to Ireland after the revocation of the
Edict of Nantes, and they still bore their French
surname. My father's people, the McClures, were
from Galloway, Scotland. The family had come
across the North Channel about two hundred years
ago and settled in Ulster.

After the battle of the Boyne, as for hundreds of
years before, it was a common thing for the Protestant kings of England to make large grants of Irish
land to Protestant colonists from England and
Scotland. Ulster, lying across a narrow strip of

1

water from the Scottish coast, was given over to colonists from the Lowlands until half her population was foreign. The injustice of this system of colonization, together with the fierce retaliation of the Irish, brought about the long list of reciprocal atrocities which are at the root of the Irish question to-day.

With such a dark historical background, the religious feeling on both sides was intense. There had been very few instances of intermarriage between the Scotch Protestant colonists and the Irish Catholics who were the original inhabitants of the Province of Ulster. Among both Protestants and Catholics the feeling against intermarriage was so strong that, when such a marriage occurred, even in my time, it was considered a terrible misfortune as well as a disgrace. This state of feeling had kept both races pure and unmodified, though they mingled together in the most friendly fashion in all the ordinary occupations of life. In Antrim the Scotch colonists had retained much of their Lowland speech. The dialect of Mr. Barrie's stories was familiar to my ears as a child.

My grandfather, Samuel McClure, for whom I was named, had seven sons. He lived at Drumaglea, on a small farm, and in addition to farming did carpentering, to which trade he brought up his boys.

My father, Thomas McClure, was working for my grandfather as a carpenter at the time of his marriage to my mother, and continued to work for him for nearly a year after his marriage, living at his wife's home at the Frocess, one mile up the county road, and coming and going to and from his work every day. In my mother's home there were many sisters and brothers, fourteen in all—my grandfather Gaston had been married twice—all farmers or farmers' wives.

My mother was a girl of unusual physical vigor and great energy, and had always done farm-work. She was able to do a man's work and a woman's work at the same time. After keeping up with the men in the fields all day, she would come in and get supper for them at night. After her marriage she continued to work on her father's farm, and my father continued as one of my grandfather McClure's workmen. It was in my grandfather Gaston's house at the Frocess that I, the first child of this marriage, was born.

When I was about a year old, my father bought from my grandfather McClure a little farm of nine acres at Drumaglea, and we moved into a home of our own. This is the first home I can remember. It was a two-room stone house, with an earth floor and a thatch roof, set on a long, gently sloping hillside, about an eighth of a mile back from the main road that ran between Belfast and Derry. At Drumaglea we were midway between these two seaports, twenty-six miles from Belfast and the same distance from Derry. Eight miles to the south of us was Ballymena, a town of about four thousand population then; and eight miles to the north, on the same road, was Ballymoney, a considerably smaller town.

This county road was one of the important facts of our lives. Not many years before my time, a man in Belfast named MacAdam had originated and introduced the method of metaling roads now commonly called by his name. All our roads were macadamized and kept in excellent condition, a very important thing in a country as wet as Ireland. Through the long, rainy winters these highways and the paved lanes that led out from them were hard and firm, even where they ran through great stretches of bog-land, such as that from which we gathered our peat. On either side of the county road, sloping back from it, were dikes about three feet high, and on these dikes grew the hawthorn hedges that marked the line of the roadright. It was along these dikes that we children, on our way to school, used to find the first signs of spring— yellow primroses, and violets of a deeper color than

S. S. MC CLURE'S BIRTHPLACE

THE ROAD TO BALLYMONEY

grow in countries where the air is less saturated with moisture.

Our cottage, though it had but two rooms and no ceiling under the thatch, was a comfortable enough dwelling. The rooms seemed large—about twelve by fifteen feet—and the kitchen served for dining-room and living-room. There was a large stone fireplace at one end, with pots and cranes, where the cooking was done. In the sleeping-room were two beds; in one slept the children—three boys of us, in time—and in the other my mother and father. This room served also as a parlor, and in it was kept the best household furniture. It was called "the room," and was never used in the daytime except when we had company. Formal visitors were always taken there and served with tea and eggs.

In that part of the country a caller can not escape tea. Even if you go to see several people in the same afternoon, you must have tea at each house. In larger houses than ours the parlor was a separate room, kept shut up all the time and used only when visitors of quality appeared. Neighbor women, who ran in for a few minutes with their shawls over their heads, and men who dropped in of an evening, in their workaday corduroys, were received in the kitchen, and talked there, seated by the big fireplace. It was no hardship to use the kitchen as a sitting-room. The cooking was so simple that, after the meal was over, there was no smell of food, and the ventilation was excellent. There was always the draught of the chimney, and the kitchen door was a half-door, that is, a door in halves, like the sashes of a window, swinging outward, and the upper half was nearly always open. The temperature was seldom low enough to make the outside air unpleasant, and on either side of the fireplace were high-backed settles to protect any one who was sensitive to drafts.

This house always seemed very fine to me; everything about it seemed interesting and beautiful and just as it ought to be. I remember asking my mother once whether there was anywhere in the world a more beautiful house than ours. The earthen floors would sometimes get out of repair and have to be filled in; but the house was warm and comfortable, and my mother kept it exceedingly neat. The yard about the house and the stable was paved with stone, so that even in the wet, soggy winters the place was never muddy, and the barn-yard was always kept clean.

My father kept on with his carpenter work after he bought his farm. He could hire men to work the fields for sevenpence a day, and use his own time to better profit working at his trade. My father was only twenty-five when I was born. I remember him as a young man with a brown beard—a rather quiet man with a gentle face and manner. We children were not at all afraid of him, for he was never impatient with us. He was naturally open-hearted and open-handed. If any one in need came to him, he would give away the last shilling in his pocket. I can remember several times when friendless women, alone or with their children, who were walking the road to some distant part of Ireland, were taken in and fed and kept overnight. We could always make a shake-down bed for people who needed shelter. Such hospitality was usual in our neighborhood; nobody thought anything of it.

My father, though he was generous, was a thrifty man, and would have got ahead in the world had he lived. After he finished the public school as a boy, he hired a tutor to come to his home and give him lessons every evening for a shilling a night. He learned surveying, in addition to thoroughly mastering his own trade. A first-rate carpenter then was able to do the work that now is divided up among several trades. My father could build a house, do the finer finishing work on the interior, and he could also build a cart and make furniture. All our furniture at home was his handiwork.

We were poor, but we were of the well-to-do poor. We were always properly dressed on Sundays. We always had hats and shoes and stockings and warm clothes in winter. We had plenty of fuel, too. On the way to my grandfather Gaston's at Frocess, the road ran through a great green bog many miles in extent. As one looked off over it from the road he could see many places where there were deep holes, some of them twenty feet deep, cut down into the bog like the shafts in a quarry, where the peat had been cut deep. Some of these holes were full of water. Every year, in the month of July, we, with our neighbors, went to the bog and cut peat for the year. It was a regular part of the farm-work, like harvesting or potato-planting, and everything else was set aside for it. It was always done in July—I suppose because the bog was drier then than at any other time of the year. In the depths of this bog were many rich fat pine roots, left there from immemorial forests and preserved in their original fibrous state. These, along with the peat, made the most excellent fuel.

Our food, like that of our neighbors, was extremely simple. Potatoes were the staple, with a sparing use of bacon and plenty of butter-milk. We did not use bread, but oat-cakes, made of oatmeal and baked on a griddle. These were very crisp and tasty when they were well made. My mother occasionally varied them with fadge, a dough made of wheat flour with an infusion of potatoes and baked like pan-cakes. Fresh meat we seldom had, but we sometimes ate dried or fresh herrings, broiling them on the tongs over the peat fire. I can remember when the use of white bread and tea began to be general among the people, and I recall hearing the old people deplore the change in food and its effect upon the teeth of the people, which at once deteriorated.

Our house was only an eighth of a mile from my grandfather McClure's, and there I had a little aunt and uncle not much older than myself, with whom I used to play. I used to run along the little lane that connected the two farms at all hours of the night and day. It was in that lane, after dark, that I remember being first overtaken by the sensation of fear. I remember first thinking that one might be afraid out there, and then thinking how glad I was that I was not; then, all at once, I was afraid, though I did not know of what. It was not of the devil that time, though I always carried in mind the feeling that I might meet him.

When I was four years old I began to go to school. That was the first important event in my life. It was then that I first felt myself a human entity, and my first clear memories date, from then. Everything before is made up of vague random impressions. The nearest National School was about a mile from our house. The schoolhouse was a well built stone building, excellently equipped. There was one room downstairs for the boys, another upstairs for the girls. In our room there were six benches, or forms, with a long desk in front of each, running from one side of the room to within three feet of the opposite side. On each of these long benches sat one class. The boys of the highest form sat on the front bench nearest the teacher. I, of course, was put with the little boys in the form at the back of the room.

I remember my distress at being put next to some very dirty children, and I remember how tired I got in the afternoon. For the first three days, toward four o'clock in the afternoon, I had a long crying spell from sheer fatigue, from sitting up on the bench, and the long hours, perhaps. I distinctly remember how kind the teacher, Mr. Boyd, was to me when these crying-fits came on, and how considerate the other boys were, big and little, not making fun of me, nor teasing me at all.

For the next six months my recollections about my school life are vague. I saw that if I learned my letters fast I would soon be able to get away from the dirty children with whom I had to sit, and pass into the next form, which I did in a few months. From then on my school life was one of unalloyed happiness. My life, the pleasant part of it, has always been made up of interests, and my school was my first live interest.

School lasted six hours a day, fifty weeks of the year, and there was only a half-holiday on Saturdays. I was always a little sad to see Saturday come around, because there were more interesting things to do at school than there were at home. I liked everything about going to school. I liked the teacher and the boys and girls. The girls were taught in classes of their own on the second floor of the building; but we all came and went and played on the road together. At noon we played in the triangular playground in front of the school, with a little brook running beside it. The boys of our school were all well mannered and likable. I do not remember any fights or quarrels. Some of my dearest friends were Catholic children. I love some of those boys to this day. We were all like brothers together.

Sometimes I walked to school alone, and sometimes with my young aunt and uncle. I always enjoyed the walk, whatever the weather. In winter the fields got soft, but the grass fields and the grass along the hedges stayed green, and there was only an occasional flurry of snow. Rain we did not mind. The roads were always firm underfoot. Potatoes were planted in March, and spring began early. When the spring flowers came on and the hawthorn hedges bloomed, the walk to school became such a delight that I could scarcely wait to set off in the morning.

Children feel such things much more than grown people know. I can remember what pleasure and comfort I took, even then, in every morning looking up and seeing the blue of distant mountains on the horizon. There was something reassuring to me as a child about that vague line of purple hills, and I thought it an indispensable feature of horizons. Some years later, on the prairies of Illinois, I learned that it was not, and I used to long for those far-away mountains very bitterly.

My eagerness to be off to school in the morning was attended by one sad consequence. I was not a strong child, and always had to be coaxed to eat my breakfast. I was never hungry for it. Eggs were a luxury and we could not afford them, but my father used to have one egg for his breakfast every morning. When he cut the top off his egg to eat it from the shell, I can remember being given that little piece of the white as a special appetizer. But usually I ate very little for breakfast. After I had set off on the road to school, however, and met other children, and wakened up to the sights and smells of the morning, then I began to feel happy and to get very hungry. With firm resolution I would open the package of oat-cake that was to serve for my school luncheon, and I would nibble a very little of it. Then I would wrap it up again. But the farther I walked the better I felt, and I would make all sorts of excuses to myself to justify another attack on the oat-cake—such as that it would be pleasanter to eat it under the hawthorn hedge than in the schoolhouse; that disposing of the oat-cake now would give me all the more time for play or study at noon; or—most improbable of all—that very likely at noon I should not be hungry at all! However I reasoned, I always ate the oat-cake, to the last crumb. The same thing happened over and over, every day, for months and years. I was always lunchless and terribly hungry at noon, and I always ate my cake on the way to school again the very next day. I enjoyed my cake, too, unless I let my conscience trouble me too much about the irregularity of my conduct.

The road to school led through a beautiful country; it ran, indeed, among those same pleasant fields of oats and beets and potatoes over which we looked out from our own door. The flax-fields, with their beautiful blossoms, were the prettiest. The linen industry is one of the principal resources of the North of Ireland, and these flax-fields, with their sky-blue flowers, were a conspicuous feature of the landscape. In August the flax stalks used to lie for weeks in ditches full of water, until the softer matter had rotted away from the fibers.

In the spring and summer we passed by great patches of yellow gorse which we called whin bushes. The road led over a fine stone bridge with a single arch, which I always liked to cross, as the stream below it was very clear. But this bridge had its terrors, too. Just beyond it there was a public house where they kept geese and very fierce ganders that used to come squawking and thrusting out their beaks at us children. We little fellows were very much afraid of them indeed. I used to look forward to those geese with uncomfortable apprehension. The next landmark on the road was a church. It was not the church we attended; I don't know that I ever saw the inside of it. But it was a fine old stone church, and the church-yard was grown up with dark, luxuriant green bushes; they may have been rhododendrons. Passing this church always gave me a sense of great pleasure.

The school-room was not quiet, as schools are

now. As you approached it you heard a hum of voices. While one form recited, the other forms studied, many of the boys going over their lessons aloud. Physical punishment was a very live fact in school then. Occasionally a boy was ferruled over the hand, and we believed that if you could manage to put two hairs from your head across your palm before you held out your hand to the ruler, the pain of chastisement would be greatly mitigated. When a boy was whipped he usually tried to stuff cloth or paper in the seat of his trousers.

The most interesting thing about school, however, was lessons. We were exceedingly well taught. The National School system was then, as it is now, one of the best in the world. Every few years each teacher in the public schools was required to spend six months in Dublin, freshening up his knowledge and receiving instruction in new methods of education. I can remember when our teacher, Mr. Boyd, went, and how none of us cared much for the substitute who took his place during his absence.

I have so often wondered in the intervening years what had become of this good and kindly man that I was very much pleased when Senator Brackett, at the time these memoirs first appeared, wrote me, "I suspect the school teacher whom you mention in your autobiography is my old-time friend David L. Boyd, still living at Mt. Vernon, Iowa." I availed myself of the hint and was rewarded by the following communication from the younger Boyd:

THE SARATOGA CLUB

Saratoga Springs, N. Y.

November 8th

"My dear Mr. McClure:—

"I picked up your October Magazine last month and began reading your Autobiography. It proved most interesting, not only because it was well written, but because I had been over the ground you spoke of, about a dozen years ago.

"The more I read, the more sure I was that your old master, Mr. Boyd, was my father, for he taught in that neighborhood and had also gone to Dublin for six months' study. When in Dublin I also saw that school, and I visited in Belfast a distant relative of my father's who had the largest national school in Ireland.

"After reading the October number, I remembered a Mr. Samuel McClure of Tecumseh, Mich., who, visited my father years ago, and hearing him say that he had a nephew or cousin who was in the publishing business in New York City.

"The day that this all happened was Sunday and I

spoke of it to Senator Brackett at the dinner table, and the result was that he wrote you.

"I had a letter from my mother saying you had written my father, and how glad he was to hear from you so I felt I wanted to write you for him.

"He fell about five years ago and broke his hip and has been very much of an invalid ever since. I'm afraid he will not be able to write you so I'm doing it for him.

"Thanking you for your kindness in writing him, I am

"Sincerely yours,
(Signed) William Walter Boyd."

Arithmetic and history were the branches liked best in that school. Working out examples was like playing a game; I never tired of it. For a long while I was convinced that long division was the most exciting exercise a boy could find.

I got up at six o'clock every morning to study my lessons. I remember that I once got up at half-past two o'clock by mistake, and it did not seem worth while to go back to bed again. I studied right on until breakfast-time. I can not remember a day when I did not want to go to school. But I used to hate to come home. It seemed dull to come back to the house and sit down to some fried potatoes that were usually a little too greasy. My feeling of the excitement and importance of the day, and of my part in it, seemed to die down as soon as I came into the doorway.

I never got over that feeling. At college everything went well with me until Friday night, and then a blank stretched before me. It always seemed a hard pull until Monday. I was never able to lay aside the interests and occupations of my life with any pleasure, and I have always experienced a sense of dreariness on going into houses where one was supposed to leave them outside. I have never been able to have one set of interests to work with and another set to play with. This is my misfortune, but it is true.

I found it very hard to get books enough to read, particularly as I could never get any pleasure out of reading a book the second time. "Pilgrim's Progress" was the exception; I was able to read that two or three times with delight. Besides that, we had at home only Fox's "Book of Martyrs" and the Bible. I remember feeling very much depressed when I finished the historical books of the Old Testament, because then the last of those exciting stories was over for me. I think I liked these Old Testament stories better than any others. They took the place of books of adventure to me. I remember, too, reading one of the Gospels through several times, and each time hoping that Jesus would get away from his enemies.

Several times a year a big box of new school-books from Dublin was left at our school. Opening those boxes and looking into the fresh books that still had the smell of the press, was about the most delightful thing that happened during the year. The readers contained excellent reading matter, and until I had read them through the new ones were a treasure.

My father and mother had once been Presbyterians, but in 1859 a revival swept over the northern part of Ireland, and they were converted to the new sect, which had no name and which strove to return to the simple teachings of the early church and to use the New Testament as a book of conduct, abolishing every sort of form. These believers had no houses of worship. Our congregation met sometimes in an upper chamber of the minister's house in Ballymena, and when I was old enough I used to walk the eight miles there with my mother. At other times the minister would come to Drumaglea and hold the services in our house or in the house of one of our neighbors.

Long discussions on religious matters were common among the neighbors, and in these a boy, if he could "argue," was allowed to take part. Infant baptism was one of the subjects most frequently discussed, and people felt very strongly about it. There was much talk, too, about men being saved by faith. The best man in the world would be lost unless he repented and accepted the sacrifice of Christ's blood, while a man who had committed crimes would, if he truly repented and believed, be saved. There was no discussion about a personal devil or a literal hell, because there was no doubt about them. If any one suggested that the torments of hell might be mental rather than physical, he was set down as an atheist without further question. I remember taking part in these discussions when I was seven or eight years old.

We heard some discussion of the Civil War, too; but our notions about it were vague. When Mr. Boyd, our schoolmaster, explained to us boys that the war was between the Northern and Southern States of North America, and not between North and South America, that was a great revelation to us.

I can remember, when I was about eight years old, going into Patrick McKeever's country store one evening, and seeing a group of men standing close together in the dim candle-light, talking in an excited way. I listened, and heard them say that

President Lincoln had been assassinated. I can remember the scene perfectly—the people composing that group, their attitudes, and the expression on their faces. No piece of news from the outside world had ever moved me so much. It was the first of the world happenings, the first historical event, that had ever cast a shadow in my little world.

Years afterward, when I was publishing Miss Tarbell's "Life of Lincoln" in McClure's Magazine, I interviewed a great many people, and I found that every one of them could remember minutely the circumstances under which he first heard of Lincoln's assassination: where he was, what he happened to be doing at the time, exactly how the news reached him. That day stood apart from other days in his life.

Every summer my mother took us children to Ballycastle, on the seashore, eighteen miles to the northeast. There, on the bay across from Fairhead, we used to take lodgings and stay for a week or so, that the children might have the benefit of the sea air. There we went bathing, and were allowed to play along the shore. I can remember, on one of these sojourns by the sea, when I was about five years old, becoming desperately attached to a young woman called Phoebe, a sister of our landlady. But after we went away I never thought of her again.

My first trip to Ballymena excited me very much. All the way there I kept feeling afraid that the city would not come up to my expectations, and I was so impatient that I thought every village along the road must surely be Ballymena. When we at last reached the place, everything delighted me—the clean streets, the neat brass signs outside the doors, the smell of soft-coal smoke—it was the first time I had ever smelled that odor so suggestive of the city—and most of all the gas street lamps, which were lit before we started for home. Those street lights seemed to suggest London, where I had always meant to go. I had thought about America, too, and that I would sometime go there in a ship. My notion of a ship was unconventional; I always imagined ships as being round, like a wash-bowl, with a mast in the center, from which ropes were stretched to the rim, and on this rim the passengers sat.

When I was seven years old my father went to Belfast to work at his trade in Harland and Wolff's shipyards. He had been away from us only a few weeks when my youngest brother, Robert, a year and a half old, died of diphtheria. After his death my father came home to see us, and stayed with us for a while. Then he went over to Greenock, in Scotland, to work on a man-of-war that was being built there, doing some of the finer carpenter work in the finishing of the cabins. I remember how sorry we were to see him go, and how we watched him from the house, as he went down our hill, across the road, and then disappeared over the next hill.

Up to this time, however, I have had very few gloomy recollections. I was always delighted at the good fortune of being alive at all, of living in such a beautiful country and such a beautiful house, of being able to go to school and of having such fine playfellows. I have spoken of the long rainy winters, but when I think suddenly of Ireland I think of blue skies, light, fleecy clouds, and glowing sun. I know there was a great deal of raw weather, but it is the memory of the pleasant weather that seems to have stayed with me. I have often noticed that after a sea voyage or a sojourn in foreign countries, people remember the fine days, but the bad weather they soon forget.

All the turns of the season were delightful to me. In winter, when we used to come home from school through the twilight, I got great pleasure out of the early nightfall and the fact that it was dark by

half-past four. That seemed to end the responsibilities of the day most agreeably, and to give one
such a long evening. In summer I always found
something exciting in being able to read out-of-doors
up until ten o'clock at night, and in the fact that
there were then only three or four hours of darkness
out of the twenty-four.

I was very conscious, too, of the kindness of
older people. I used to wonder about it, and to
think how remarkable it was that they should
make allowances for all my peculiar shortcomings,
and that they always treated me so nicely. This
feeling that the world all about me was friendly to
me was very distinct, and it counted for a great
deal in my life. I suppose I was an optimistic child,
for I was always confident that delightful things
were going to happen, and I never believed that
unpleasant ones would, or even thought that they
might. On my way home from school I was always
imagining that when I got home I would find a
splendid surprise of some kind, that something
wonderfully nice had happened to the house or to
my mother, or was waiting for me. One of my
favorite anticipations was that when I got home and
ran into the house, I would find a beautiful lady
sitting there—quite a story-book sort of person, a
lady of quality, radiantly lovely and magnificently

dressed. But I was never downhearted when these things did not come true.

What did come true was something I had never even believed possible.

One November day, when I was nearly eight years old, I was going home from school in very high spirits. I had then been at the head of my class in every subject for seven weeks, and I was feeling that my father would be very proud to hear this. My class, moreover, was the highest in the school, and my classmates were big boys, fourteen and fifteen years of age. It usually took a boy more than a year to get through a form; but I had started to school when I was four years old, and in three years I had got into the sixth form, doing two forms a year. I found it exciting to stand at the head of a class of boys nearly twice my age, and I tried hard to keep my place at the head—though I remember reflecting that this was a low motive for trying to do well in my studies.

On this November day I was coming along the home road with several other boys, and we were all feeling unusually gay. We stopped at a turnip patch beside the road, where there were Swedish turnips, very sweet and not at all bitter. We were all hungry, and we went into the field and began to eat turnips with great enjoyment. While we were laughing and talking, a man came along the road, and called out to me:

"Samuel, your da is deid."

I left the turnip patch and started home, but I had no clear realization of what the man meant. When I got home, I found neighbor women there, looking after the younger children and the house. My mother and my grandfather McClure had gone to Glasgow to my father. Father had finished his day's work on the war-ship, and was leaving the vessel to go to his supper and then to the prayer-meeting. Through the carelessness of one of the workmen, a hatch had been left open that was supposed to be kept closed. In leaving his work my father fell down this hatchway, from the deck clear to the bottom of the hold, and seriously injured the base of his skull. He was taken to the infirmary at Glasgow, and died within three days after his admission to the hospital. My mother and grandfather did not reach the infirmary until after his death.

In 1890, when I was visiting Professor Henry Drummond in Glasgow, I went to the infirmary, and found the record in the books there of my father's admission to the hospital—"Thomas McClure, injury to the spine"—together with the number of the room in which he was put; and after looking at the books I was shown the room in which he died. He was thirty-two years of age at the time of his death.

I do not remember any funeral service. I remember that my father was brought home, I remember the coffin standing in the living-room, and the neighbors coming in to see my mother. I remember thinking then about my father's visit with us after the baby died, and about the day he went away, down our hill and over the next, and trying to realize that the look I had of him going over the hill was the last sight I would ever have of my father. The coffin was not opened. When it was taken away from the house, neither my mother nor we boys went to the interment.

It was after my father died, while his body was still in the house, indeed, that I began for the first time to be conscious of the pressure of poverty. It was not that we were desperately destitute or in immediate need, but the bread-winner of the family was gone, and I was conscious that we were facing difficulties. I knew that my mother was worrying, I could see that in her face. I remember, while my father's coffin was in the house, going out on the road and hoping that I would find just sixteen pennies in a row there, to take to my mother. It seemed to me that they would solve her difficulties.

Two months after my father's death my youngest brother was born. My mother named him Robert after the little boy who died. We suffered no serious privations, but another baby added to my mother's cares and perplexities, and there was the feeling of hard times in the house. I used to notice how at night, when we were going to bed, my mother would keep looking toward the window. I took it for granted that she was thinking of my father, and indeed it seemed to me that I might at any time see his face there, pressed against the pane. It took me a long while to realize that he had really gone away from us for good. I did not cease to miss him for many years. After we went to America, when I was a boy of fifteen or sixteen, going to the Valparaiso High School, I used to waken up in the night and cry from the sense of my loss.

My mother stayed on at our old place at Drumaglea for a year, and managed the farm herself. She was a thoroughly capable farmer, but when we were deprived of my father's wages the farm of nine acres was simply too small to support a woman and three boys, and pay the rental, and the hire of a man to help with the work. At the end of a year, therefore, my mother sold the farm back to my grandfather McClure for £100 (five hundred dollars). My father had paid only £50 for it when he bought it, but under careful farming the land had risen in value. Then there was nothing for my mother to do but to take her four boys and go back to her father's house. My grandfather Gaston died when my mother was a young girl, and my grandmother and the younger boys lived in his house at the Frocess. There we were not very happy. My mother was troubled about the future, and I was transferred to the Frocess school, where I never felt at home as I had at my own school. In the new school I did not get on so well in my lessons. I was homesick all the time for my old playmates and my old schoolmaster. Nothing about the new school seemed as nice as the old one was.

Naturally, in my grandfather's house there was a good deal of discussion as to my mother's future and what she ought to do. Her brothers thought it very unpractical to try to keep the family together. Their feeling was that we children had better be separated and parceled around among our aunts and uncles, and that my mother should stay on at my grandmother's house and work, as she had when she was a girl. But my mother would not hear to this. Before everything she would keep the family together.

My mother felt that she had not received all that was due her in the distribution of her father's estate. One morning in the early spring she and I walked to Clough, about three miles from the Frocess, to consult a lawyer. When my mother heard what steps it would be necessary for her to take to attempt to recover what she thought was due her, she decided not to enter upon such a controversy. We left Clough in low spirits, as we saw now no way of bettering our condition. On our way home we stopped at the Clough graveyard, where my father and little brother were buried. There was but one grave, for when my father was buried my brother's grave was opened and the little coffin containing his body was placed on top of my father's coffin. Coming home from Clough that day, my mother and I sought out this grave, and there, in our discouragement, we sat down and cried.

It was soon after this that we first began to talk of going to America. Mother then had two unmarried brothers and two married sisters living in Porter County and Lake County, Indiana, and she thought that in America she could make a living for herself and her boys.

We began to read steamship circulars and to consult railway maps, and soon we began to make actual preparations for the journey. My mother had some little money left from the sale of our farm.

It was, of course, something of an undertaking for a widow with four children—the eldest nine years old—and very little money, to start across the ocean to make her living and support her boys in a strange land.

We took passage on the *Mongolia*, a vessel of four thousand tons owned by the Allan Line. I remember that my mother bought cloth and had new suits made for us boys. When we started on our journey we took the train at Glarryford, and I remember the scenes of parting at the Glarryford railway station. There were a good many people from our part of the country going on the *Mongolia*, and their fathers and mothers had come to the railway station to bid them good-by. The old women wept as if they were taking a last farewell of their children. Indeed, statistics show that many of these Irish immigrants never see home again. I often think how much heartbreak each of our incoming steamers from Ireland or from Italy represents. For the old people at home such partings are like death.

In our case there was no bitter grief. My mother was of a hopeful nature. She was then a strong young woman of twenty-nine, and was confident that she was doing the best thing for her boys. We were to sail from Londonderry. When the train swept around a curve and ran alongside Lough Foyle, the water seemed to me to rise in a slope beside us. We got off the train, and were put into a tender that carried us out of this Lough, twenty-six miles to the open sea, where we got on board the *Mongolia*, which had sailed from Glasgow.

We sailed on Friday the 14th day of June, 1866, when I was nine years old. Our steerage quarters were comfortable. We were not crowded, and the food was good. The first two days and nights we were all seasick and very miserable. I lay in my bunk Friday night with a raging thirst. I was too ill to get water, and nobody else was well enough to get any for me. I remember dreaming that I was drinking cool buttermilk in my grandmother Gaston's milkhouse at the Frocess. By Sunday, however, we were well enough to be on deck. I found everything delightful, and greatly enjoyed playing on the clean decks. All the way across I had a singular illusion which I have never since had at sea; it seemed to me that the surface of the water was concave, shaped like a bowl, that the vessel moved at the bottom of this concavity, and that the water swelled on all sides and met the sky.

We were to land at Quebec. I can remember going into the Gulf of St. Lawrence and then into the St. Lawrence River, and the never-to-be-repeated sensation of approaching the coast of a foreign land for the first time. Although this is an experience that one can never have twice, I had somewhat the same feeling, years afterward, when I first saw Jerusalem. We had sailed from London-derry June 14, and we landed at Quebec June 26. The railway journey from Quebec to Valparaiso, Indiana, took seven days. Our immigrant train would be held up for hours on a side-track while passenger trains and even fast freights passed us. We bought our food as we went along, changing our English money as we had need. We were delighted to find that we got seven or eight dollars in exchange for a gold sovereign, but we were astonished to see how fast these dollars slipped away when we came to buy food. Everything, of course, was dearer than at home.

We reached Valparaiso on the third day of July, 1866. I suppose we were all very tired by this time, for I do not recall much about our arrival. My uncle, Joseph Gaston, met us with a wagon, and drove us fourteen miles south of Valparaiso to the farm where my mother's sister, Mrs. Coleman, lived.

The next day we drove to Hebron, two miles away, and there I celebrated my first Fourth of July

in America, had my first firecrackers and lemonade.
The exercises were conducted in a grove, where
there were wooden seats and a speaker's platform.
The orator of the day was Mr. Turpie, who was then
the Democratic candidate for Congress. I remember feeling that he and I were of opposing parties.
I don't know how or when I became a Republican,
but I landed at Quebec nine years old and a ready-
made Republican. Mr. Turpie, in his speech,
voiced the sentiments usually expressed on such
occasions. He talked about the land of freedom,
of popular institutions, and unbounded opportunities. I had never heard such a speech before. All
these sentiments were new to me and moved me
very deeply. As I sat in the grove listening to this
speech, I could see off across the country, as far as
my eye could reach, a great stretch of unfenced
prairie in place of the little hedge-fenced fields I
had always known. My heart swelled with the
swelling periods of the orator. I felt that, as he
said, here was something big and free—that a boy
might make his mark on those prairies. Here was
a young country for Youth.

"EVERY YEAR, IN JULY, WE WENT TO THE BOG AND CUT PEAT FOR THE YEAR"

S. S. MC CLURE, ABOUT THIRTEEN YEARS OLD
(FROM A DAGUERREOTYPE)

S. S. MC CLURE, ABOUT TEN YEARS OLD (FROM
A TINTYPE)

CHAPTER II

MY MOTHER'S COURAGEOUS EFFORTS—MY
MOTHER MARRIES AGAIN—I ATTEND SCHOOL
IN WINTER—MY WORK ON THE FARM—VAL-
PARAISO HIGH SCHOOL—I WORK AS A CHORE-
BOY—CHARLEY GRIFFITH—MY RESTLESSNESS
—I TRY FOR A COLLEGE EDUCATION

ALTHOUGH my spirits rose so high on that
Fourth of July day in Hebron, our arrival in
America was the beginning of very hard times for
my mother and us boys. We were now almost
entirely without money, and were staying with my
mother's sister, Mrs. Coleman. Her husband was
struggling along on a little rented farm. He had
then half a dozen children of his own, was living in
a small story-and-a-half frame house, and my two
unmarried uncles, Joseph and James, who had come
over the year before, were living with him. To
have a woman and four children arrive to share these
already overcrowded quarters was a serious matter.

Very soon my brother Robert and I were sent to
stay with another married sister of my mother, who
lived north of Valparaiso, and my mother went to
Valparaiso and got a place as servant in a household

there. My aunt's husband was having a hard struggle to get along, and he soon became tired of having two extra children quartered upon him. So one day, without warning, he hitched up the wagon and took my brother and me to town and handed us over to mother. My mother was working for the Buell family, living in their house, and when her brother-in-law drove away her position was embarrassing. What to do with her two children she did not know. She could not very well ask the Buells to take us in. Late that afternoon, as evening was coming on, we wandered about the town with her, wondering what we should do. We came to a brick block called the Empire Block, on one of the business streets, which was undergoing repairs and was then unoccupied. Here we found an empty room that was open, and here we spent the night.

In order to keep us with her, my mother decided to give up her place at the Buells' and do washing by the day. For a dollar a week she rented a room in this same Empire Block, and here we lived, my mother, my youngest brother, and myself. My mother obtained washing and ironing to do in four families; so four days a week she went to the houses of these people, doing all the washing and ironing for a family in one day, and receiving $1.75 for a day's work.

Later Doctor Everts' wife, who had probably heard of my mother's efforts to get along, came to her and told her that she would gladly let her have one of the downstairs corner rooms in her house for herself and her boys, if my mother would do the family washing. This proved a very satisfactory arrangement for us. We were most kindly and hospitably treated in the Everts family. They were extremely considerate of my mother and of us children. Dr. Everts had a large library, and for the first time in my life I found myself in a house where there were plenty of books. I sometimes read two or three books a day. I lay on the carpet, face down, and read for hours at a time. It was then that I first read "Robinson Crusoe."

In that library there were some books about witches and witchcraft which I eagerly devoured. They took possession of my mind and made me so unhappy that I have always felt that such books should be kept away from children. I remember thinking that any one might be a witch in disguise, and wondering whether my own mother were not. I was so nervous that, when some children came in one evening with their faces blacked and grown people's clothes on, I ran screaming into the yard, and could not be quieted for a long while.

But these easy times, too, came to an end. The

Everts family moved to Indianapolis, and then we found ourselves back in my uncle Coleman's over-crowded story-and-a-half house, fourteen miles south of Valparaiso, with winter coming on. My mother could always get work if it was to be had, and she obtained a place six miles away from the Coleman farm; but she received only two dollars a week, and this was the period immediately following the War, still remembered for the high cost of living. Brown sugar, I remember, went up to twenty-five cents a pound, and gold was at a high premium. I remember the great anxiety about getting shoes for the children. I had gone barefoot as late as possible, like all the other country boys, and delighted to do it; but the time came when shoes were a necessity. My mother managed to get them, somehow. I can remember when she bought me mine, and that they had brass toes. We had not very heavy clothing, and during that winter we children and the Coleman family lived very meagerly. I remember the hard-ship of having to eat frozen potatoes boiled into a kind of gray mush. I did not thrive on this nourish-ment. Before the winter was over I had become so weak that my hands were very unsteady and I could not carry a glass of water without spill-ing it.

Half a mile west of us lived Thomas Simpson.

His farm was the outlying farm of the neighborhood, the one nearest the unoccupied land where the cows grazed. Simpson was a kindly, industrious man from Tyrone, Ireland. He wanted to marry my mother. Clearly something had to be done, and it seemed to mother that when she had this opportunity she ought to marry and give her children a home. She married Thomas Simpson that winter, and Robert and I were taken to his house. The other two boys lived a while with Mr. Simpson's brother, but my brother John came to live with us in March.

There were a hundred acres in the farm, and it was worth about three thousand dollars. At the time of his marriage to my mother Mr. Simpson owed five hundred dollars on it. During the several years that I worked on the place we were never able to reduce the debt. Sometimes we fell behind and owed money to the storekeepers in Hebron.

John and I did the morning and evening chores, which I always hated. The work I liked was cutting wood for the kitchen stove. Our stepfather got his fire-wood from the Kankakee swamp, a great stretch of marshy land to the south of us, of considerable geographical importance in that country. There were wagon-roads through the swamp, and when it was frozen over the settlers took their teams in and felled and hauled away their winter wood. The timber was mostly ash, which is easy wood to split. John and I cut up and split ten logs a day. The logs were about ten feet long and eight inches to a foot in diameter, and each log made six lengths of stove wood. As long as I stayed on the farm I enjoyed this work. Some years later, when I was working my way through college and doing pretty much everything that came to hand, I suddenly turned against wood-sawing. I made up my mind that I had sawed so much wood that, whatever happened, I would never saw any more. And I never have.

The second winter I attended school for the first time since we came to America. I went to the Hickory Point School, and my Irish speech afforded the boys there a great deal of amusement. The snows were very deep there, and the crust was often so hard that we skated to school, over fields and fences. I was so fond of school that, if I had to work at home for part of the day, I would go all the way to school to get the last hour, from three to four, there.

When I was twelve years old and was still going to that school, I heard somewhere, for the first time in my life, that there was a kind of "arithmetic" in which letters were used instead of figures. I knew at once that I must somehow get hold of this. I asked the teacher, a young man who was then trying to work his way toward a medical school; but, though he had heard of algebra, he had never studied it and had no text-book. There lived not far from us an ex-soldier named McGinley, and I had heard that his wife had been a school-teacher. I went to Mrs. McGinley to ask her advice, and she lent me an algebra. My brother John and I took up this book and went through it as fast as we could, working it out for ourselves and solving the problems as we came to them. We got so excited about it and talked about it so much that my stepfather said he thought he would like to study it, too. He would sit down with us in the evening and work at the problems. But after a little while his zeal flagged and he decided that he could get through the rest of his days without knowing algebra.

During these years the lack of reading matter was one of the deprivations which I felt most keenly. We had no books at home but a bound volume of "Agricultural Reports," sent us by our congressman, and this I read over and over. Then I used to read, with the closest attention, the catalogues sent out by the companies that sold agricultural implements. They seemed absorbingly interesting, and I read them through like books. When I was about thirteen years old I first read, in the weekly edition of the Chicago *Tribune*, "The Luck of Roaring Camp." It seemed to me a fairly good story about an interesting kind of life. Petroleum V. Nasby, the famous dialect philosopher of that time, I read closely in the weekly paper. It was then I first began to hear of Mark Twain, and to see little extracts from him quoted in the newspapers. It was years before I saw even the outside of one of his books.

I remember some hunters once camped for the night on our place. I went over to their camp the next morning after they were gone, and found that they had left several old paper-backed novels and a few tattered magazines. These were a great find for me. Years afterward, the idea of forming a newspaper syndicate first came to me through my remembering my hunger, as a boy, for something to read. In the early eighties, when I was working for the *Century Magazine* in New York, and was going over the files of the *St. Nicholas Magazine*, I could not help feeling how much I had missed. Here were good stories of adventure, stories of poor boys who had got on, stories of boys who had made collections of insects and butterflies and learned all about them, or who had learned geology by collecting stones and fossils—things that I might have done, myself, if I had known how. It occurred to me that it would be an excellent plan to take a lot of these stories from the old volumes of *St. Nicholas* and syndicate them among the weekly county newspapers over the country, where they would reach thousands of country boys who would enjoy them as much as I would have if I had had them. I took this plan to Mr. Roswell Smith, of the Century Company. Mr. Smith did not carry out the plan, but the idea of such a syndicate was firmly fixed in my head, and later I was able to carry it out myself.

After I had started my newspaper syndicate, I did manage to get Stevenson and Kipling, Conan Doyle, Stanley Weyman, Quiller-Couch, Stephen Crane, the new writers and the young Idea, to the boys on the farm. I am always meeting young men in business who say: "Stevenson? Oh, yes! I first read 'Treasure Island' in some newspaper or other when I was a boy. It came out in instalments"; or "Why doesn't Quiller-Couch ever write anything as good as 'Dead Man's Rock'? I read that story in the Omaha *Bee* when I was a kid, and I think it was the best adventure story I ever read. I never got the last chapter. Our paper didn't come that week, and it bothered me till I was a grown man. I finally had to get the book and find out what did happen to Simon Colliver." I believe that my newspaper syndicate did a good deal to awaken in the country boys everywhere an interest in the new writers of that time, and to create for those writers an appreciative audience, besides all the pleasure such stories gave to minds that would have been emptier without them.

The second summer I spent on my stepfather's farm—I was eleven years old—I did the same work as a man, except where my lack of height was against me. I built the hay on the wagon, for instance, instead of throwing it up from the field, and when the hay was forked from the wagon I built it up on the stack. John and I planted the corn by hand, dropping across the plowed furrows. We cultivated the corn twice, twice down the rows and twice across. When I was twelve and thirteen years old a part of my work was to break the young colts to being ridden.

We all worked hard, but it seemed to me that my mother worked hardest of all. She got up at five every morning and milked five or six cows. The North of Ireland people are the best butter-makers in the world, and when butter was bringing twelve and a half cents at the stores in Hebron, my mother's butter always brought twenty-five cents a pound and was sent to families in Chicago who had given a standing order for it. Besides milking and making butter for market, my mother did all the housework, the cooking and washing and ironing and caring for the children. During the seven years that my stepfather lived, my mother bore four children, of whom three died in infancy of enlargement of the spleen. I seem to remember that there was always a sick baby in the house. About the time the new baby was a few weeks old, the eighteen-months-old baby would fall sick, and then my mother would have a baby in her arms and a sick baby in the cradle. She did a great deal of her work with a baby in her arms, and often after being up half the night with the sick one. I used even then to wonder how she did it.

My stepfather was always kind to us. Though physical punishment was then regarded as a necessary thing, especially for boys, he never whipped any of us. He let us work, indeed, harder than growing boys should have been allowed to work, but it was because he knew no better. All our neighbors worked their boys, and my stepfather himself worked very hard. No matter how hard we worked, we could never seem to reduce the debt that we still owed on our farm. The summer that I was fourteen my mother got discouraged. She had always had a fierce desire that her boys should be educated, and my schooling was at a standstill. I had gone as far

as I could go in the country school, and had done all
the work several times over. I had worked beyond
my strength all through the summer of my fourteenth year. Haying was late, and the heavy work
came in the very hot weather. I used to drop on
the ground from weakness after my work was done,
and I suffered so from dysentery that I was unable
to sit on the buggy-rake.

One day in September, my mother called me to
her and told me that she could not see any chance
for me on the farm. If I wanted more education I
must manage to get it for myself, and the best thing
for me to do was to go away and try. At Valparaiso
a new High School was to open that fall, and my
mother said she thought I had better go there and
see if I could work for my board and go to school.
I followed her advice.

I carried with me no clothes except those I had on,
and I don't think I took a package or a bundle of any
kind. I had no capital but a dollar and the hopeful-
ness and open-mindedness of fourteen years. When
I came out on a little hill above Valparaiso and
looked down at the white houses and the shady
streets, bordered by young maple trees, I had a lift
of heart. It seemed to me the most beautiful place
in the world.

I walked into Valparaiso as fast as I could, and

began going from house to house, asking whether anybody wanted a boy to do chores and go to school. It was then late in the afternoon, and I had to get a place to sleep that night. The Everts family, for whom my mother had worked, were then living in Indianapolis; but I went to some of their neighbors. Some one told me that they thought Dr. Cass would take a chore-boy. I knew of Dr. Cass. Indeed, once, when he came to our farm to buy corn, I had computed in my head the cubic contents of a crib for him.

Dr. Cass was then the richest man in all that country. He owned several farms and a good many cattle, and was worth something like $100,000. He was reputed a hard man and was not very well liked. I went to his house and he took me in. There I was called at five every morning, made the fire in four stoves, took care of the cow and the horses, and did part of the marketing before school. In the afternoon I worked on the grounds and did chores until supper-time, and after supper I studied my lessons. Every Monday, however, I was called at one o'clock in the morning to help Ida and Bertha, the two daughters of the house, with the washing. By eight o'clock we would have the washing for the family on the line.

As I have said, there had been no High School in

Valparaiso until that year. It was conducted in one large room of the new school building just completed.

After the new pupils were seated, Professon McFetrich came down the aisle, asking each boy to give his full name and say what studies he wanted to take. I was a little nervous, anyway, and it made me more nervous to hear each boy giving three names—John Henry Smith or Edward Thomas Jones. What bothered me was that I had but two names, Samuel McClure, and I didn't want to be conspicuous by having less than the other fellows. I began to rack my brain to supply the deficiency. I had read not long before a subscription history of the Civil War, and had greatly admired the figure of General Sherman. Professor McFetrich was still about six boys away from me, and before he came to my desk I had decided on a middle name. So, when he put his question to me, I replied that my name was Samuel Sherman McClure. Later I changed the Sherman to Sidney. I am usually known now as S. S. McClure, but there never was any S. S. McClure until that morning, and my becoming so was, like most things in my life, entirely accidental.

After he took down my name, the principal began to name over the studies, for me to say "yes" or "no": Arithmetic, History, Latin, Geography, German, Algebra, Geometry. To his amusement, I said "yes" to every one of them. I did not know what else to do. There was certainly nothing in that list that I could afford to give up, and it didn't occur to me that I could save any of them and take them at a later date. During the morning, however, I began to get nervous about the number of studies I had agreed to take. At noon I went to the principal and told him that I was afraid I had registered for more subjects than I could do justice to. He smiled knowingly and said he thought I had. We compromised on a rational number.

I had come to Valparaiso run down and worn out with the hard summer on the farm, and the work at Doctor Cass' was not light for a boy of fourteen. Still, I got on pretty well except for the fact that I had no money. I had my board and lodging from Dr. Cass, but not a penny to buy clothes or books. Of course I had no overcoat. I didn't own an overcoat until I was nearly through college. When it was cold—and it was often bitterly cold—I ran. Speed was my overcoat.

I stayed with Dr. Cass through the first term of school, and then I went to spend Christmas with my uncle James Gaston, who had married and then lived four miles north of Valparaiso.

I was not supposed to be away from my chores for more than a day or two, but I had not had a vacation for a long while, and I had such a good time at my uncle's that I overstayed my time. The snow was hard and firm. Sleighing was fine, and there were a lot of friendly young people about. There was one very pretty girl, Helen McCallister, with whom I thought I was very much in love. I certainly enjoyed that vacation. But when I went back to Valparaiso on the first day of January, Dr. Cass refused to take me in again, because I had overstayed my time.

My misfortune, however, was only temporary, and my loss proved to be my gain in the end. I soon heard that Mr. Kellogg wanted a chore-boy. John and Alfred Kellogg were brothers who lived in a double house in Valparaiso and, with a third brother, operated an iron foundry. I went to live with the Alfred Kellogg family, and there I found a home indeed. I at first joyfully characterized the house to myself as a "place with only one cow and one stove." And Mrs. Kellogg was so merciful to the sleep of growing boys that she frequently got up and made that one fire herself. I regret to say that I can remember lying guiltily in bed on a cold morning and hearing her build it. I could never adequately describe the kindness of the Kelloggs.

I finished my first winter at the Valparaiso High School happily enough in the Kellogg family. When the summer vacation came on, it was necessary for me to get something to do. I passed the county examinations, and took charge of a country school two miles north and east of my stepfather's farm. I received fourteen dollars a month and boarded round. I had an opportunity to find out how bad country cooking in America can be, and what outrages can be committed upon good food-stuff.

The custom was then in country schools to keep the little children in their seats all day, although they had only three or four recitations during the school period. This seemed to me inflicting a needless hardship, so I decided to give the youngest children eight short recitation periods a day and to let them play out of doors the rest of the time. The doors and windows of the schoolhouse were always open, and I could keep an eye on the children just as well as if they were inside, squirming in their seats.

This was not the usual way of managing a country school, however, and a hired man who worked in the fields near the schoolhouse complained to the directors that the new teacher didn't teach the children anything; he was sure of this, because whenever he looked up from his plowing he could see children playing in the yard. I can remember the look of that fellow; he was a big man with a big, brutal face, and for years afterward, whenever I read about bullies or ruffians in novels, they always took on the face of that man.

The school directors met and asked me what I had to say to this charge. I was then fifteen, had had no experience in teaching before, and I was so amazed I hadn't anything to say at all. On the contrary, I put my head down on the desk and cried. But Mr. James Carson, one of my old teachers at the Hickory Point School, spoke up for me, defending my conduct, and the charge was dismissed. I could not, however, teach out my term of three months. The humdrum of teaching was more than I could endure. At the end of two months I quit. One thing I could never do was teach a country school. I tried it twice afterward, but both times I had to run away from the job before the term was over.

The next winter I went back to Valparaiso to go to school. A friend writes recalling how I found much needed help from Mr. and Mrs. T. M. Shreeve.

"Many times have I heard them tell how Uncle

Tommy, one frosty autumn morning, when driving into Valparaiso from his marsh farm, overtook a boy in the road and asked him to ride. Upon inquiry as to his destination the boy replied that he was going to Valparaiso to attend school, but he did not know whom he was going to see there. Uncle Tommy took the boy to his house and kept him. He did chores mornings and evenings, and clerked on Saturdays and holidays in Uncle Tommy's grocery. I have heard Aunt Hattie tell how she used to sit up nights to knit stockings for him to wear to school."

This winter I had to have more clothes and more school books. I seemed to need more money than I had the winter before, and my school work was interrupted more by the necessity of earning it. I clerked in Mr. Shreeve's grocery store for two months, and for two months I was printer's devil for the proprietor of the Valparaiso *Vidette*. I learned to set type and make up the paper, but what I most remember was learning to swear. Profanity was then the accepted etiquette about a country newspaper office. The oaths meant nothing. They were not even ingenious or amusing, and they were not indicative of strong feeling. It was simply an ugly habit, like tobacco-chewing—which I got to hate there because the loafers in the office used to spit on the floor about the type-cases, from which I often had to pick up type. I soon became expert in profanity myself, and could scarcely utter a sentence without an oath. When I got over this habit of swearing, I got over it entirely. Ever since it has seemed to me a vice as stupid as it is ugly.

I have always been against using profane expressions in McCLURE's MAGAZINE, except where the author could convince me that they were absolutely necessary for the truthful portrayal of character— and then the author had to be some one who knew what he was talking about.

About this time I fell in with Charley Griffith, a lad of my own age who lived with his widowed mother on a hill at the edge of the town. Charley didn't go to school; his eye was too much on the main chance, and he was exceedingly full of shifts. Charley was a great schemer. He was always devising novel and interesting ways to make money. He was never afraid to work, but somehow he never stuck at anything long and he never came out much ahead. Charley's large and adventurous ideas took hold of me right away. Credulity was my native virtue; I beamed with it.

It would take me a long while to enumerate all the ventures upon which Charley and I embarked with proud hopes. I remember at one time we used to borrow horses, ride about the country all night until

we could find some one who had an old cow for sale
cheap, lead her home, and butcher her in a disused
slaughter-house outside the town. Then, after cutting the meat up, we would sell it off a wagon about
the town. I can't remember that we ever made
much. I dont' know what ever made Charley think
he could be a butcher, unless it was seeing a perfectly
good slaughter-house that nobody was using, and
figuring that if only he could be a butcher, he would
be ahead a slaughter-house. Charley often figured
his profits on a similar basis.

When the summer vacation came on, we decided
that it was time we entered business in earnest. I
was then sixteen and Charley was about the same
age. We went to Westville, a small town about
ten miles from Valparaiso, and opened a butcher
shop. We started out with a flourishing business,
and sold all the meat we could get. It looked a sure
thing from the first, and we felt pretty well fixed and
had a great sense of dignity. I remember what good
breakfasts we used to get at the restaurant near our
shop, and with what complacency we ate our pork
chops and coffee. But at the end of the month our
dream was shattered. We sent out our bills, " dr.
to meat for one month," with great satisfaction, but
we received few replies. Then we learned that most
of our customers were "dead beats," people who

owed the other butcher shops so much they couldn't get any meat there. Some of them had not had any meat for a good while, so they had bought it on a generous scale when they had a chance.

Well, now we had no meat and no money. Charley's ardor cooled. We decided that we would employ our talents in other fields. We sold all we had except our team and wagon, and Charley suggested that we drive to Anderson, Indiana, and get a job grading where the Baltimore and Ohio Road was being put through. I was game for that too, so off we went.

But again we were poor calculators, for there were two of us and we had but one team. We got a job on the grade, but there was an extra boy with nothing to do. I drove the team, while Charley tried to get a job carrying water. We worked on the grade for some weeks, and I have forgotten now just why we left it. Probably the elusive goddess beckoned Charley in some other direction.

As for me, I have never been sorry that I tried and learned something about a good many kinds of work when I was a boy. If I had become a writer when I grew up, such knowledge as I obtained from these experiences would have been of inestimable value to me. The late O. Henry was one of a dozen writers who got their material and their knowledge of people and of the caprices of fortune by knocking about at all kinds of jobs. I am not sure but that, in another way, such experiences were almost as helpful to me as an editor. They made me, I think, more open-minded than I would otherwise have been, and more quick to recognize the young writers who were trying to tell the truth about some phases of American life.

In the fall of '73, when I was sixteen years old, I went back to Valparaiso, and went to work in the Kellogg iron foundry for four dollars a week, living with the Kelloggs again and paying them two dollars a week for board. That was the panic year, and times were so hard that I couldn't manage to start to school at all that fall. Money was so scarce and so hard to make that I became discouraged and began to think of throwing up everything and taking to the road as a tramp.

The life of a tramp would not have been so distasteful to me as it would to most people. I escaped being a tramp so narrowly that I have always felt that I know exactly what kind of one I should have been. I don't think I should have been unhappy as such. After I left the farm and first went to Valparaiso to go to school, I began to have attacks of restlessness. I simply had to run away for a day, for half a day, for two days. It was not that I wanted to go anywhere in particular, but that I had to go somewhere, that I could not stay another minute.

These fits were apt to come on at any time; but in the spring, when the first warm winds began to blow, then they were sure to come, and to come with a vengeance. There was no standing up against them, and there was no punishment like trying to stand up against them. Usually I didn't try; I simply ran down to the station and took the first freight-car out of town. I rode until I was put off, and then maybe I waited until I could catch another outbound freight and rode some more. Maybe, if the first passing freight happened to be headed for Valparaiso, I jumped on it and rode home. I ran away like this, not once or twice, but dozens and dozens of times. It was a regular irregularity in my life. It was, indeed, more than most other things, a necessity of my life. I could do without a bed, without an overcoat, could go without food for twenty-four hours; but I had to break away and go when I wanted to.

In those days, on each freight-car there were two little platforms about a foot wide, one at each end of the car, where the brake-rod came down. On this little projection I used to sit, with my cap pulled down tight on my head. Of course I preferred to ride on a passenger-train, and I usually managed to get out of Valparaiso on a passenger, resorting to freights to get home. When I rode on the passenger, I made myself at home on the blind end of the baggage-car, winding my woolen comforter close about my neck to protect me from the showers of sparks that blew back from the engine.

This restlessness was something that I seemed to have no control over. I have had to reckon with it all my life, and whatever I have been able to do has been in spite of it. As a lad I followed this impulse blindly, but later I realized that this restlessness was a kind of misfortune, and that it could be at times a hard master. In most things I was fickle and inconsequential, open to any suggestion, ready to quit one job because another was offered, not a very good judge of business propositions, the plaything of casual contacts and chance happenings. But there was one fixed determination, one constant quantity, in my life as a boy— the desire to get an education. That was my one steadiness. Everything else was as it happened. In reality, my runaway trips, my rushing from one job to another, were only apparent ficklenesses. The one thing I really meant to do was to get an education, and in that I never wavered.

In December of 1873, while I was working at the

foundry and wondering what I was going to do next, I received a message from my mother telling me that my stepfather was very ill and I was to return home at once. I went home, and in a few weeks my step-father died of typhoid fever, leaving the farm to my mother and their one living child. I was mother's oldest son, and there was nothing for me to do then but to stay at home and work the farm for her.

My brother John was then fifteen and my brother Tom thirteen. Robert was still a little fellow. So that winter my two brothers and I undertook to run the farm. In the spring we planted the crops, and that summer we raised and harvested the largest ones that had ever been produced on that farm. In addition, we increased our profits by taking over some marsh-land and making hay on it on shares.

It was while we were working in the hay-field, one day, that there occurred one of those seemingly un-important events which are often destined to make a great change in people's lives. My brothers and I saw some one coming across the hay-field, and as he approached we recognized my uncle Joseph Gas-ton, whom we had not seen for several years. He was trying to fit himself for the ministry, and was then attending Knox College, at Galesburg, Illinois. He came up to us in the field, asked us about the farm and how we were getting on with it, and then told us that the thing we must try for was a college education, and that the place to get it was Knox College.

Since I first left the farm to go to school I had meant to get to college somehow; but how I should go, or to what college, was not clear to me. As I listened to my uncle, this vague project instantly became a definite plan. I was going to Knox College. Uncle Joseph talked the matter over with my mother, who required little persuasion. She wanted all her boys to have an education, and, as I was the oldest, it was natural that I should have the first chance.

When September came I set off for Galesburg with eight dollars to pay my carfare, and a heavy black oilcloth valise. Because of this valise my money did not hold out. I took the train at Hebron, and when I arrived in Chicago I had to pay a man fifty cents for hauling me and my big satchel across the city from the Pennsylvania depot to the C. B. & Q. depot. When I went to get my ticket to Galesburg, I found I had not quite enough money left; I hadn't counted on that fifty cents. I bought a ticket to Galva, a town about twenty miles this side of Galesburg, and trusted to luck. I went through all right.

I got off the train with fifteen cents in my pocket. I had on my only suit of clothes, and my mother had made them. The trousers were a good deal too wide and about an inch too short in the leg, and of very stiff cloth. The coat and vest probably had similar faults, but I was most conscious of the trousers. I had on a pair of cowhide boots, and a black felt hat with a droopy brim. I went at once to the campus, and stood looking over the campus and the buildings. I thought I had never seen such fine trees. The afternoon was singularly fresh and clear after a rain, and everything looked wonderful to me.

There are few feelings any deeper than those with which a country boy gazes for the first time upon the college that he feels is going to supply all the deficiencies he feels in himself, and fit him to struggle in the world. My preparation had been scanty and I would have to enter the third preparatory year; that meant that it would be three years until I was even a freshman. I was seventeen, and it was a seven years' job that I was starting upon, with fifteen cents in my pocket. I felt complete self-reliance. I had never had any difficulty in making a living, and I knew that I was well able to take care of myself. On the first afternoon, certainly, there was no room in my mind for apprehensions. I could only think about what a beautiful place this was, and that here I was going to learn Latin and Greek.

Once in Ireland, when I was a little boy, in the Public House at Ballymena I had seen a young priest sitting at a table, reading a book intently. I looked over his shoulder, and, though I could read very well by that time, I could not read a word of that book. I asked him why this was, and he told me that this was Latin. I had never heard of Latin before, but I instantly knew that I wanted to learn to read it, and resolved that one day I would. Now, ten years later, on the other side of the ocean, that day had come.

CHAPTER III

Knox College—Working My Way as a Farm-
hand—Teaching Country School—Greek
the Most Important of My Studies—My
return to Ireland when I Was Nineteen—
Restless for America—I Determine to
Ship as a Stow-away—My Letter to the
First Officer—Working My Passage as
Mess-Boy—My Engagement—A Winter in
Which I Nearly Perished of Cold and
Hunger—My Dismal Meals with The
Divinity Student

KNOX COLLEGE is situated in the heart of the
great corn region, in one of the most fertile dis-
tricts of the fertile Middle West. Although I
arrived there without resources, I knew that food
was plenty and cheap. Such being the case, I felt
sure that I would get through college some day.
The first thing to do was to get a place in which
to stay until I could find work, and I set out to find
my uncle, Joseph Gaston. On the college campus
were two dormitories known as "the Bricks," low,
one-story brick structures, one on either side of the
main building. In one of these buildings my uncle
shared a room with another student.

During the first month I lived on bread and grapes varying this with soda crackers and grapes. I could get three pounds of delicious Concord grapes for ten cents. I found an unrented room in the dormitory building, perfectly empty except for a box. In this room I studied that first month, and there I ate my meals, keeping my supplies hidden under the box. I've forgotten how I arranged for a place to sleep.

At the end of a month I got a place with J. C. Stewart, then mayor of Galesburg, to work for my board. I lived in his house for the rest of the year, and was in every way treated like a son. I earned extra money for books and pocket-money by sawing wood about town. During the winter my mother sent me money enough to buy a suit of clothes to replace my home-made suit, which was half worn out when I left the farm. Beyond this I had no outside help at all; and at the end of the school year I had made my own way, and had six dollars left.

Of course, I knew that I would have to work in vacation; so, when examinations were over, before the Commencement exercises, I got on the train and rode to Wataga. There I struck off into the farming country, picking my way along the sod beside the muddy roads. I worked all that summer as a farm-hand. The first job I got was grubbing out a locust grove. I grew very lonesome at this kind of work, and asked the farmer, after several weeks, whether I couldn't work overtime for a few days and then get half a day off to go to town. He told me that there was no way of making up time on his place—that all my time was paid for, and so there wasn't any overtime. This was true of farm-hands in general then; a man had no time that he could call his own.

When I got the locusts grubbed out, the farmer passed me on to his son-in-law. Here, besides doing the chores and milking, I plowed all day. That plowing was a little different from any I have ever done. This young farmer had a most remarkable team of horses. They were so strong and full of spirit that they would trot in the plow. I could not hold them back. So every day we plowed three acres instead of two, the amount a man usually plowed in a day. Any farmer will realize that this was pretty hard work. I used to get up in the morning so stiff and sore that I could scarcely walk from the house to the barn, harness my horses, and then off on the trot. In the field I soon got limbered up, but by night I was a tired boy. I got the usual wages of a farm-hand at that time, twenty dollars a month.

Toward the end of the summer, before the college

term opened, I went back to Indiana to visit my mother, and stayed with her for a few days. On my way back to Galesburg I had to spend a few hours in Chicago. Walking along the street, I stopped before a cheap clothing store and looked at some suits of clothes that were displayed in the window. The proprietor came out and simply worked a suit of clothes off on me. I did not know how to resist his importunities, and to buy the clothes seemed the only way of escape. I paid twenty dollars for the suit, and it wore out in a few months. That unwise purchase helped to put me behind in funds. Before Thanksgiving my money was all gone, and I saw that I would have to leave school until I could make some more.

I got a country school near Dwight, Illinois, and went to teaching about Thanksgiving time. There I was marooned in a perfectly flat prairie country, a most depressing sight in winter. Illinois roads are proverbially bad in winter, but that season there was a rainfall even heavier than usual. The whole country was like a sponge and the roads were simply impassable. The school term lasted only four months, but after three months I simply had to throw up the job. I couldn't stand the dullness and the flatness and the wetness of the country any longer. When I got back to Galesburg, it seemed the finest place in the world. I had kept up my studies in my absence, and now went on with my class.

A word about the college curriculum. Four-fifths of the students at Knox then took the old-fashioned classical course, in which Greek was obligatory. This course still seems to me the soundest preparation a young man can have, and I still feel that Greek was the most important of my studies. During the years that he reads and studies Greek a boy gets certain standards that he uses all the rest of his life, long after he has forgotten grammar and vocabulary.

I enjoyed Greek and mathematics more than any other subjects I took at college, and Homer more than anything else we read in Greek. After I began Homer, I used always to give four hours to the preparation of the next day's lesson, my best study hours, too—from six to ten in the evening. I looked forward to those hours all day. I went so far as to write out a vocabulary of the first book of Homer, giving, with the help of Liddell and Scott and Curtius' Etymological Dictionary, the Latin, German, and English equivalent of each word. This exercise made the succeeding books easy reading. About this time I read Professor Whitney's book on "Language and the Study of Language" and Trench's book "On Words," books of a new kind to me.

PROFESSOR ALBERT HURD

MRS. ALBERT HURD AND HER DAUGHTER HARRIET WHO AFTERWARD
BECAME MR. MCCLURE'S WIFE

Of college life, in the sense in which it is now used, there was then none at Knox. There were no fraternities, no organized athletics, no student dances, no concerts, no students' orchestra or glee club. All the students were earnest, and most of them had had a hard time getting there. A boy's standing among the other boys depended entirely upon his scholarship, and every one did his best. We were allowed to take only three college studies at a time, and we had three one-hour recitations a day. There was no sense of drive or hurry. On the contrary, one felt that Knox College was a place set apart for boys to grow strong and to develop in mind and body. One felt no pull of the world there, but a kind of monastic calm. In seven years I scarcely read a newspaper.

The three strongest men in the faculty of Knox College then were Professor George Churchill, Albert Hurd, and Milton Comstock. Professor Churchill was at the head of the Preparatory School, and it was he who took the green boys that came in from the farms and directed their efforts. He had such a love for humankind in general, and for boys in particular, that he could awaken ambition in the dullest and give confidence to the shyest. He became the friend and encourager and inspirer of the boys in their first and hardest years at school.

Professor Comstock was at the head of the department of mathematics, and his scholarship was much respected among the boys. Professor Hurd was nominally head of the Latin department, but he taught other subjects as well. He was generally recognized as the most accomplished scholar in the faculty, and as one of the greatest natural teachers the country then possessed. There are never too many of these at any time.

To give the reader a better conception of this splendid scholar, I quote the words of Professor Willard as given in "The Story of Knox College —Seventy-five Significant Years," by Martha Farnham Webster.

"Now I come to one who for fifty-five years was an active professor at Knox and doubtless did the most to determine the character of its instruction, and to put his impress upon the intellectual habits of its students—Professor Albert Hurd. 'Noblest Roman of them all,' has ever been our involuntary tribute. . . . The gifts, the culture, the disciplined power, the ardor and the devotion that he gave to the college of his heart, can be spread upon no canvas, can find no portrayal in words. Clean cut as a cameo were his features, but the expression of his thought had the definiteness of outline and the distinctness of projection of a mathematical figure. His expression was clear and vivid because his own conception was so, and his command of speech, his lively imagination, his chaste taste found evermore the fitting word. Truth with him was something sacred, and his temperament was volcanic so that no student cared to trifle either with the truth or with the Professor. But intense as were his feelings, strenuous as were his labors, his energies seemed never to tire, never even to flag. His physical powers seemed able to meet any strain he might make upon them. During a large part of his life he was doing the work of two or three men, and yet when he was past middle age he made the remark that he did not know what it was to be tired.

"That which was most characteristic of Professor Hurd was his absolute unselfishness toward the institution to which he had consecrated his life. The fact has been mentioned that he was often doing the work of two or three men, but for this he would accept no more than his meager salary; and if the trustees insisted upon giving him additional compensation, it was accepted only on condition that it might be used for improving the equipment of the institution.

"Neither were Professor Hurd's services confined to the college. The community shared the benefit of them as truly as of Prof. Churchill's. Before I

72

had become a student in Knox, my imagination
had been quickened and my appetite for knowledge sharpened by Prof. Hurd's popular lectures
on geology. He, too, was a most acceptable
teacher in the Sunday schools. Any history of the
Galesburg Public Library should bear upon its
frontispiece a portrait of Professor Hurd with the
title Albert Hurd, Founder of the Galesburg Public Library. For years, and without salary, Professor Hurd was librarian of the Young Men's
Library, the care of which the city later assumed
as the Public Library."

The ardor and unselfishness of his devotion to a
chosen purpose were a renewal of the character of
his great-grandmother, Barbara Heck, justly called
the founder of American Methodism. "The first
structure of the denomination in the Western hemi-
sphere"—the old John Street Methodist church, of
New York— "was a monumental image of the
humble thought of this devoted woman."*

By the time I finished my second preparatory
year, my mother had sold the farm for between three
and four thousand dollars, and, as all of her boys
were pretty well able to take care of themselves, she
decided to go home to Ireland to visit her people.
As I was the oldest son, she took me with her. We

* History of the M. E. Church, by Stevens, Vol. 1, page 63.

left Galesburg on June 6, 1876. The Centennial rates were on then, and we went from Chicago to Philadelphia for $11. There we stayed for some days with relatives, and went to the exposition. As I remember the exposition, the telephone exhibit, which was certainly the most important thing there, attracted little or no attention, while people crowded around the butter statue and things of a like nature.

On June 15, 1876, we sailed from Philadelphia on the *Illinois*, American Line. When we reached Liverpool, we found a lodging-house where we got lodgings for ninepence a night. After we were rested from the voyage we took a boat for Belfast— always a most disagreeable passage—and from Belfast we took the train to Glarryford. I had left Ireland when I was nine years old, and I was now nineteen. Nineteen is a fine age, and Ireland is a fine country. I have never forgotten that ride from Belfast to Glarryford. It was a beautiful day late in June, with brilliant sunshine and a sky intensely blue, and everywhere the wonderful green of Ireland, like no other green in the world. I could see, as it were, the cleanness of the grass, washed by so many rains. The whole countryside presented the look of neatness and tidiness that I had always missed in Indiana and Illinois. The white houses, plastered and graveled outside and then whitewashed, glistened in the sunshine, and the rose bushes were everywhere in bloom about the doors. I noticed the rich green of the boxwood hedges about the gardens, and the dark laurel bushes which I had always loved when I lived among them.

The train seemed to go very slowly. The fields looked very small, of course, to a boy who had been a farm-hand in the great corn country of the West; but they looked very restful, too, and well kept behind their green hedges. Many of the country people were out weeding in the potato and beet fields that morning. Most of the early wild flowers were gone, but here and there on stony hillsides the yellow gorse bushes were in bloom.

After mother and I alighted at Glarryford, we went at once to visit my mother's brother, Samuel Gaston, at the Frocess. In the immediate neighborhood there were twelve or fifteen families of Gastons and McClures, and we visited about from one to another, calling on our old friends and neighbors as well. I was struck by the industry and thrift of the country people, and by the dignity of respectable competence. Every one seemed to have his place, and to enjoy filling it as well as he could. One felt everywhere the peacefulness of a long-established order.

S. S. MC CLURE AT THE AGE OF NINETEEN

S. S. McCLURE'S HOME IN WHICH HE LIVED UNTIL HE LEFT IRELAND

I spent a good deal of time with my grandfather McClure. He was then an old man, and he had never got over the loss of his son. The affection he had felt for my father he seemed to transfer to me, and I think he got great pleasure out of my visit. Before I returned to America he begged me to stay in Ireland. I told him that I would come back some day, but he said he would not live to see that day—and, indeed, he did not.

My grandfather, as I remember him, was an irascible man, very positive in his prejudices, religious and social. In his younger days it had been a hobby of his to object to young men of the neighborhood who came courting his daughters, and tales of his violent physical attacks on yearning swains were current in my day. I have recently received a letter from a Mr. William Ramsay of Salem, New York, who has given so many facts concerning my grandfather and his surroundings that it seems appropriate in this place to give an extract.

SALEM, WASHINGTON CO., NEW YORK.
Jan. 28, 1914.

"I cannot forbear writing to express the pleasant surprise to me to find that the "Story of a County Antrim Boy" which is appearing in the Ballymena Observer is the story of McClure of the popular magazine of that name, and that especially you are from Drumaglea, County Antrim. My name is William Ramsay, who, in 1872, was the means principally in the building of the Baptist Meeting House and parsonage in Clough. Before that I was preaching in Ballymoney. When one Pat Wilson of Drumaglea visited me and came to one of my meetings in Ballymoney, I was then invited to preach at Wm. McClure's of Drumaglea, brother of your grandfather, Samuel McClure. From that day the little assembly that had formerly met in Wm. McClure's met there no more—they decided to attend my meetings in Ballymoney. And from one Lord's day to another Pat Wilson, one Pat Miller, Wm. McClure and his wife with their three daughters, Mary, Matilda, and Margaret—with the members of four or five families from Clough, walked down to Ballymoney. Some of them came twelve miles. Then through the meetings held in and about Clough and Drumaglea, the membership grew till the time came for the expressed desire to arrive and build, and for me to make Clough the center. You will have seen the buildings when over in Ireland in '76. Although I was holding evening meetings at Wm. McClure's at the time of your visit I do not remember your being there. Perhaps I can account for this from the fact that your grandfather, who was a very strong Presbyterian in principle, was so bitterly opposed to Baptists, so called, that he not only prevented his immediate family from attending my meetings, but he would not even speak to his brother William.

"But Samuel took sick and I visited him. All were surprised at his receiving me and harkening to the simplicity of the Gospel spoken by me. From time to time there were more marked changes in him, both in mind and in the failure of the flesh. And being of necessity absent for about three weeks, on my return to Clough I found a note from the family, saying that Sam was dead and he had requested me to preach the funeral sermon, which I did." . . .

As I went about among our old neighbors, watching the field work and the peat harvest, people talked to me a great deal about my father, in a way that moved me greatly. He had been a man much trusted and beloved by his neighbors, and his sudden death at the age of thirty-two had caused genuine sorrow there. The people talked about him as if he had been dead only a short while, and they told me many things about him that I have always been glad to remember.

There are, of course, always certain disappointments attendant upon going back to the country that one left as a child. I remember how bitterly disappointed I was upon going back to my old school, which throughout the ten years since I had left it I had remembered with so much pleasure. My old schoolmaster had gone away, and the school itself seemed to have gone away. At least, the school I remembered was no longer there. Everything seemed so different that I could not feel that it was the same school at all.

Although I was glad to see Ireland again, and had such a good time visiting among my relatives and greeting old neighbors, I soon began to feel very restless. My mother had decided that she would not take me back to America with her, but that I should go to work either in Ireland or England and make my living there. As for me, I wanted to go back to Galesburg to go on with my college course. Moreover, I had then met Harriet Hurd, who eventually became my wife, and I was very much in love.

Miss Hurd's father was Professor of Latin at Knox, and Harriet herself was that year a senior. We had corresponded since I had been away from Galesburg, and, though my letters from her were not many in number, I managed to spend a great deal of time reading them as I wandered about the fields. At last I became too restless to stay still any longer. I wanted to get away, where I could be alone and where I would not have to talk to my relatives or to any one else.

One day, unencumbered by any luggage, I struck off across the country toward the east coast. Before I reached it, I had to cross the line of purple hills which I used to watch from the door of our house when I was a child. These hills are a good deal like those in the Highlands of Scotland, and were covered with pink and white and purple heather. As I climbed them, the farm-houses grew fewer and fewer, until at last I was quite alone amid the heather. This was exactly what I had wanted, and I felt a great relief. The quiet was so absolute that I would hear my watch ticking away in my pocket, and before the day was over that watch seemed like a pleasant and unobtrusive companion. I felt as if it were alive and conscious.

I was gone on this tramp for two weeks. I walked from Larne to the Giant's Causeway down the rugged coast, nearly always keeping the ocean in view, and wondering how I was going to get across it. I had then two shillings and odd pence, but I spent very little of this on my tramp. Wherever I went, the people refused money. They gladly kept me overnight to hear me talk about America. In the late afternoon I would come to a house, and see some children playing in the yard, and a pleasant-faced woman leaning on the half-door and looking out at me with curiosity. I would stop and tell her where I came from and who I was, and ask her if she could give me some supper and a place to sleep. By nine o'clock I would be asleep in the bed with those same children.

The shore-line along that coast is steep and corrugated granite cliffs, with the turf growing down to the very edge. I remember I narrowly escaped a tumble of five hundred feet when I was crossing Fairhead Mountain. It was a particularly pleasant time to be adrift on the road, for the hay-making was going on, and it was a dry season. I do not think it rained once during those two weeks. I remember the pleasure of coming suddenly upon a little glen, with hay-fields on the hillsides, and a village tucked away by the stream down in the valley. I have gone on a great many tramping expeditions in my life, both as a boy and as a man, in the Alps and in the Michigan woods, through Illinois and Indiana, and among the Great Lakes; but I have never enjoyed any tramp as I did that one in Ireland, the summer I was nineteen.

When I got back to my relatives at the Frocess and Drumaglea, I had determined that, by some means or other, I would get back to Galesburg.

My perplexities never long remained a secret to those about me, and I suppose that in a few days all my relatives knew that I was bent upon going back to America, and that I had no money. At any rate, when I got up one morning, and went about from house to house to tell my aunts and uncles good-by, each of my uncles gave me a present, some a sovereign, some a half-sovereign; so that by the time all my good-bys were said I had about thirty dollars. I went to Belfast and from there to Liverpool. In Liverpool I found the lodging-house where my mother and I had stayed six weeks before. The *Illinois* was in dock, preparing for her next trip to Philadelphia. In those days a steamer lay in dock ten days after every crossing, and was ten days going and ten days coming, so that she made the round trip in thirty days. At that time it took a fleet of six ships to keep weekly sailings. I had made up my mind to return on the *Illinois*, and to return without paying my fare.

It would, I knew, be useless to try to get a berth to work my way across; there was a dullness in shipping just then, and many hands were being laid off. With the port full of experienced men looking for a job, there was no chance for a green hand, so I decided to stow away. While the boat was outfitting, I went on board several times a day and talked to the baker and several of the stewards, with whom I had become acquainted on the way over. I told them frankly what I wanted, and they said they guessed they could fix it all right. I suppose they were hoaxing me, but I had not the slightest doubt that they meant what they said and that everything would be easy. As I have said before, credulity was my native virtue.

When I was not hanging round the ship's docks, I sat in my room at the lodging-house, eating penny buns and reading penny dreadfuls—the kind that Stevenson said were "a penny plain and tuppence colored"—listening with pleasure to the interesting noises of a strange city. After living so long in the Middle West, the inflections of the English speech, and particularly the fresh voices of the children, seemed delightful to me.

One day when I was on board the *Illinois*, talking to the baker and the stewards as I got a chance, I was unfortunate enough to attract the attention of the first officer. I was wearing a gray linen hat, and that helped to make me conspicuous. The officer called out, "Come here, boy! I mean you with the light hat."

I went up to him, and he said, not roughly but in a very final way: "I've seen you about here before. Now, I want you to get off this boat, and stay off."

I went on shore and sat on the dock in the deepest dejection. I simply had to cross on that boat. I bought some writing-paper, and, sitting on the docks, I wrote the first officer a long letter, telling him that I simply had to cross on his boat; that I had to get back to America to finish my college course; that when I got through college I was planning to go to a medical school and study to be a doctor. I don't know what made me tell him all this, though it was perfectly true: that morning I did intend to become a doctor. I got one of the seamen to take this letter to the first officer, and I sat on the dock, overcome by despondency.

I had no idea that my letter would have any weight with the officer, or that I should ever hear from it again. I had written the letter to relieve my own feelings; I had no hope that it would influence his. Indeed, the fact that I had written the first officer a letter had almost passed from my mind, when the officer himself came to the side of the vessel and beckoned to me. I went on board, and he spoke very kindly and said that he would see that I got to America; that he would take me over as a helper to the ship's doctor— this, of course, in deference to my professed ambitions. We had not been twenty-four hours at sea before the doctor discovered my utter unfitness for any such job. It happened that the officers' mess-boy had a felon, so I was made mess-boy, to do the work under his supervision.

The officers' mess-boy, my superior, was a very clever fellow. During our passge over on the *Illinois* I had often noticed him and admired his accomplishments. He sang very well indeed, and danced clogs in a really remarkable fashion. He used to sing and dance on the steerage deck, to the great delight of the passengers.

As mess-boy, I had to work for my passage indeed. We left Liverpool in a storm, and for the first three or four days the vessel was on her beam-ends most of the time. I had to get up at five o'clock in the morning, and take rags and a pail of suds and scrub out the corridors. When the boat was pitching, the corridor was like a bowling alley, and my pail and I were bumped first into one wall and then into the other, up and down, back and forth. Seasickness added to the precariousness of this work. I had, of course, had no breakfast, but the cook gave me a cup of coffee before I began to scrub, and I remember with gratitude that the coffee on that boat was excellent. By eight o'clock

I had breakfast laid for the officers, ten places in all, and I served the breakfast. Lunch again at twelve, etc. I had to wash all the dishes, and for the first four days, when I was very seasick, this was disagreeable work.

One of the mess-boy's duties was to make pastry, not only for the officers' mess, but for the cabin passengers as well. This I soon learned to do very well. I baked fifty pies every day. I would have my stewed fruit ready, of course, before I began to make the crust. Then I took a large dish-pan and filled it with cracked ice and water. In this I put the butter, and left it there until it became as cold and hard as it could possibly become. I then put the mass of butter on the rolling-board, worked the flour in rapidly with my hands, rolled it thin, cut out the lower crust, placed it in the pan, filled it, placed on it the upper crust, slashed this across the middle, and then dented it around the edge with a fork. Making good pastry is such a simple operation that I have often wondered why there are so many poor pies in the world. The most important thing is to have the butter very cold, and about this I believe many cooks are careless. I did not mind making pies; but when, on Thursdays and Sundays, I was required to freeze ice-cream in addition, I thought people were a little unreasonable and that they would not demand ice-cream if they knew how much trouble it was to make it. On the whole, I thought the ten days of that crossing stretched out very long.

Whenever I was not doing anything else, I had to polish the brasses. I had no time off duty except an hour from four to five in the afternoon, when I used to crawl up on deck and sit still very limply. My berth was next the smokestack, and was so intolerably hot that nobody could have slept there, even on the most comfortable bed. And that bed was the worst I had ever seen. When I lifted the mattress, the under side of it was brown with cock-roaches, alive and dead, spread as evenly as if they had been put on with a paint-brush. When I went off duty, at eleven o'clock at night, after arrang-ing the officers' midnight lunch, I took my blanket, lay down in the hall, and got such sleep as I could until I had to fall to work with my scrub rags and pail at five.

When we got to Philadelphia, I was asked to stay on board for a few days and help the men who were unloading the vessel. The first officer told me that I would lose nothing by being obliging. I didn't lose anything, but I didn't gain anything, either. I didn't get a penny for my pains. How-ever, I was not sorry that I had obliged the officers.

The first officer was a fine man, and I respected him. Ten years afterward, when I was in Philadelphia on business, I tried to find him. I learned with regret that he had been accidentally killed on a shooting expedition along the Chesapeake.

From Philadelphia on, I had to pay my fare. When I got back to Galesburg on the 7th of September, I went up to the campus, and met a lot of the boys I knew. There was a new building going up, a gymnasium. All the students were contributing something toward the new building, and they were all very much excited about it. Until that time student enterprises had been few. I got off the train at Galesburg with exactly one dollar in my pocket, and this dollar I at once gave to the gymnasium fund. I thought I might as well start even.

As soon as I got rid of my dollar I went to call upon Harriet Hurd. I had met her only six times before I went to Ireland, but our correspondence during the summer had ripened our friendship. When I went to see her after my return, I asked her whether, if I turned out to be a good man, she would marry me in seven years. She said that she would, and I went away feeling that the most important thing in my life was settled. But, like many another boy, I was to learn that such arrangements between young people are often very far from final, that outside powers can intervene very potently, and that such settlements can be to the last degree unsettling.

It is necessary to explain, perhaps, why Miss Hurd's parents and friends felt that her friendship for me was very undesirable. Although in actual age there was only a year between us, Miss Hurd was then a senior at Knox, while I was not yet a freshman, being only in the last year of the preparatory school. A brilliant and beautiful girl, Miss Hurd not only led her classes, but had reached a higher average of scholarship than any student who had graduated from Knox up to this time. The old system of exact grading then obtained, and it was many years before another student equaled Miss Hurd's record. As a girl of very unusual promise, the daughter of the ablest man in the faculty, she held a unique position in Galesburg. She had behind her a background of calm and culture as different as possible from the vicissitudes of my early life. Professor Hurd and his wife naturally looked with disfavor upon their daughter's attachment for a rough country boy who had already a reputation for being visionary and unstable, and who had certainly no very encouraging prospects. I felt that their opposition was reasonable and yet intolerable, and it was this feeling that made matters go so badly with me that winter as they did.

That winter of my twentieth year I let myself very nearly perish from cold and insufficient food. I say "let myself," for of course I was always perfectly well able to make my living, and had done so many kinds of work that I could turn my hand to almost any sort of employment. Up to this time I had rather enjoyed the shifts by which I got along on small sums of money, and the readiness with which, when I needed books or clothes, I could go out and turn up a job. But now certain kinds of work that I had always done became hateful to me.

All through my life, there have been milestones at which I simply got through certain kinds of work. I got to one of these milestones in the winter of 1876–77. I told myself that I had got through sawing wood and tending furnaces, and I had got through doing chores. I had always hated chores, and I had been a chore-boy since I was eleven years old. Now my patience was exhausted. I detested currying horses, for instance; I hated the dust and the hair and the smell; and now I had come to the place where I simply couldn't take care of stables any more. To this day "chore" is to me the most hateful word in the English language. I am sure that thousands of country boys share my detestation of it. Chores are to country boys what dish-washing is to country girls—a dreary, drudging routine that hangs over the most cheerful day. So that year I struck, so far as chores were concerned; and hard times came of it. But, in whatever straits I found myself, it did not even occur to me to relieve the pressure by turning to the odd jobs at which I had once been so handy. When I went to bed supperless, there was no question in my mind, "Shall I go back to chores?"—none whatever. I had finished all that kind of work; it had ceased to exist for me. It was as if I had absolutely forgotten how to take the clinkers out of furnaces, or had never known how; as if I had never seen a furnace, or a stable, or a wood-pile.

In so far as my college work went, that year opened up brilliantly. By this I mean, not that I did anything brilliant, but that the studies I took up that fall were more engaging and interesting than any I had had before. We began Virgil's Æneid, which I read with the greatest delight as a story of adventure and romantic love. I suppose it was the first time my imagination had been greatly stirred by anything in print, and I had reached an age when one's imaginings begin to be colored by one's personal feelings and are more alive than the fancies of childhood. I used to feel for hours together as if I were actually along with Æneas and his companions, wandering about the blue Mediterranean. The Æneid, naturally enough, set me to hunting for other books of a romantic flavor. I read Jean Paul Richter's "Titan" and Goethe's "Wilhelm Meister." I also discovered Carlyle and Emerson.

When the first snow fell in late November, I was wearing a straw hat. It was not so much the time that I spent in reading these books that made more practical occupations impossible to me, as the mood which they induced. Less than ever did I want to poke the clinkers or milk the cow. I was full of all sorts of new impulses, but none of them led to the stable or the saw-buck. And safety, for a poor boy like me, lay with the cow and the wood-pile. Instead of hustling about as I had always done, I read and studied most of the day, and in the evening I walked about the town and the fields and the woods, preferring the dark and the stillness to the company of the other boys.

Of course, it was very illogical in me to adopt this mode of living when I needed money as much as ever. But life is illogical. I believe that most people who believe that their lives have moved according to a plan, carefully made and consistently followed, deceive themselves. There are exceptions, but caprice and chance have their way with a good many of us.

The winter began in November, and was one of the coldest I have ever known. I had a room in "the Bricks" that winter. This building was only one story high and one room wide, so that I was at once on the ground, under the roof, and between two outside walls. The cold was evenly distributed on the four sides of my cube. There was a fireplace, but until the 13th of December I had no coal at all. Then Harriet Hurd had a birthday, and her father gave her five dollars for a birthday present. She gave this money to me, and with part of it I bought half a ton of coal. That was the only coal I had during the whole winter.

Nearly every night the pail of water in my room used to freeze solid and swell up in the center. I had a fur cap by this time, and I used always to eat my meals walking up and down the room, with my cap and woolen mittens on. I seldom had anything to eat but bread, and it froze so hard that it was full of ice and hard to chew. I can not remember anything more dismal than those meals in that terribly cold room. A very poor divinity student roomed with me for a few weeks—a solemn, pious fellow with protruding teeth; and I remember, one Sunday when we came home from church and had nothing but cold corn-meal mush for our Sunday dinner, he varied his usual blessing as we confronted the dish, and said: "O Lord, bless, we pray thee, this miserable food to our perishing bodies."

Going to bed, however, was the greatest hardship. The sheets were so cold, and had been cold for so long, that getting into bed was like plunging naked into a snowdrift. At night I usually studied in the public library, or in the office of the hotel, or in the waiting-room of the depot, where there was always a red-hot stove. Though we were not to read those authors until the next year, I set about making a vocabulary of the first book of Homer and the twenty-first book of Livy. Doing this sort of work in the evening, I thought, would make me sleepy. But, on the contrary, I became more and more wakeful. Lack of nourishment probably had a good deal to do with my wakefulness. But the idea of going hungry was much less repugnant to me than the idea of hustling about and hunting chores to do. I got so that I could go to bed supperless without feeling any great discomfort. I knew plenty of people who would have been glad to give me a good dinner, people with whom

I had often had dinner when I did not need it. But when a boy is really hungry it is difficult for him to go out to dinner. There is something about it that makes him unnaturally shy. My theory, when I first came to Galesburg, was that nobody could be hungry in a place where food was plenty and cheap. I now found that supposition to be a mistake. The reason was purely psychological. I couldn't bring myself to ask for this food which was so plentiful.

The year wore on to spring, and the Commencement exercises took place toward the end of June. I had never stayed for the Commencement before, as I had always been off a few weeks before school was out, hunting for work. But this year Harriet Hurd was among the graduates, the valedictorian of her class.

Perhaps because of her part in the Commencement exercises, perhaps because they were the first I had ever seen, they seemed very impressive to me. The little procession, headed by the trustees, in which the graduates marched across the campus from the main building and down the street to the Opera House, seemed to me very solemn. Although the ceremonial aspect of the Commencement was so slight, it served to make me feel that there was a long distance between a graduate student and a freshman.

The exercises took place in the morning. That afternoon I gathered a bunch of pansies and took them to Miss Hurd's house. She was in the parlor, with her father and mother and several of her relatives. When I was shown in, I felt at once the chill in the atmosphere. Professor Hurd was a very frank man. He always showed me plainly that he did not like me, and on that afternoon his greeting was very cool. None of the others were any more cordial. Usually, the more embarrassed I felt, the harder it was for me to take my leave and get away; but that time I managed to get away very soon. I gave my pansies to Miss Hurd with the best grace I could under such hostile supervision, and, after a few awkward moments, escaped.

After Commencement was over, I was still hanging on at my room in "the Bricks." I do not know why. With no means of self-support in view, I was still working away at comparative etymology and making up my Greek and Latin word-books for the next year. I had by this time a thick manuscript book. I have no very clear recollection of that period. I worked a little every day, but I grew weaker all the time. For some reason, probably for coolness, I had put my mattress on the floor, and I used to lie there and study. Some one told Mr. Bangs, whose wife was principal of the girls' seminary, that I seemed to be in a pretty bad way, and he came over to my room and looked me over. My appearance must have confirmed the report, for he at once got a buggy and took me over to the seminary. I was put in one of the empty bedrooms there, where his wife could look after me. I was so weak that for several days I could take no nourishment but toast water.

With proper food I recovered rapidly, and on the 10th of July I went to call upon Harriet Hurd. She met me at the door in tears, and told me that her father was going to send her away to school, and that she had promised him not to see me again or to write to me. I said good-by to her on the porch, and went down the path. I did not see her or hear from her again for four years and two months, though I do not believe that she was out of my mind for a single day during that time. I had then not the least hope that she would ever marry me, or even that I would ever see her again. My feeling for her became a despairing obsession, as fixed as my longing to get an education had been. During the rest of my years in college, I used to look every week at the list of marriages in the

Galesburg *Register*, always fearing to find an announcement of Miss Hurd's marriage to some one whom I did not know.

As fall came on, and it was time for me to begin my freshman work at college, I decided to leave Knox and go to Oberlin and enter there as a freshman. It seemed to me that I would get on better in a place where there would be no disturbing memories and associations. If I stayed at Knox I would be in Professor Hurd's classes. I felt his disfavor keenly, and seeing him served to keep my troubles fresh in my mind. I realized that for a boy in his freshman year heartaches were a serious disadvantage. I had my trunk packed, when my uncle Joseph Gaston, who had been my mentor before, convinced me that this would be a very foolish change to make and that working my way in a strange town might hold me back.

During my freshman year I heard nothing from or of Miss Hurd except once. As I was going down the corridor of the main college building one day, I heard Nan Bateman, the president's daughter, ask Professor Hurd where Harriet was. He replied that she was at Berthier, on the St. Lawrence, studying French. I had never heard of the place, but I dashed upstairs and got an atlas in which I soon found Berthier-en-Haut, where there was a French Protestant school for girls. I at once wrote Harriet a long letter and sent it to that address, but I received no reply. Years after I learned that my letter did not reach her.

CHAPTER IV

I got through the winter of my freshman year
at Knox College without serious privations. One
reason for this was that I paid more attention to
my way of living than I had the winter before.
I was not much distracted, and became more sys-
tematic in my way of providing for myself. I did
not earn much more money than I had the winter
before, but I made good use of what I got. I lived
in a room in the Bricks, and prepared my own food,
as before; and that winter I bought soft coal at
three dollars a ton, and had heat the winter through.
This also enabled me to have hot food, which was a
great advantage.

I became a fairly good cook that winter, and I learned the last word in cheap living. I got sixteen bread tickets for a dollar, and each ticket was good for one loaf of fresh bread or two loaves of stale bread. As I usually bought stale bread, I got thirty-two ten-cent loaves for a dollar; this was getting a value for my money that it would be hard to beat. I used to go to the butcher shop and get for nothing the ribs and other bones that the butcher had cut out of the meat and thrown under the counter. These, boiled in water, with a little beef tallow, made a soup that was palatable, if not very nourishing.

Potatoes I bought for twenty-five cents a bushel. After giving them a rough wash, I used to slice them very thin and fry them in hot tallow. I believe the best hotels now follow that method, frying potatoes raw instead of boiling them first. Sometimes my food did not cost me more than eighteen cents a week. Then, again, I would get reckless, and would live high, spending as much as seventy-four cents a week.

I came out at the end of my freshman year in good spirits and in fairly good condition, and began to look about me for some way of making money during the summer. In most occupations, except farming, fewer hands were needed in summer than

in winter. Farm-hands were paid only twenty dollars a month then, and the work was heavy for a
boy of slight build who had never been overly well
nourished. Besides, to get worked down during
the summer, and come back to college in the fall
thin and tired, as I had been when I entered the
Valparaiso High School, seemed bad economy. My
desire to find a new kind of work plunged me into a
series of adventures and experiences that were all
wholly unexpected and unforeseen; one thing simply
led to another.

The story of that summer's adventures begins
with Mr. Bangs, the man who took care of me the
year before, when I had absent-mindedly starved
myself weak.

Mr. Bangs had the misfortune to seem funny
to every boy in school. He was a small, neat little
man, somewhere between fifty and sixty, with very
correct manners and a very exact way of speaking.
His wife was principal of the Girls' Seminary, and
he lived there because his wife did. He had no
position, no salary, and, though he used to help
his wife, whatever he did was regarded as officious,
for he had no right to do anything. He attended
to the kitchen and dining-room for his wife. In
the dining-room of the Seminary some of the students were boarded, boys as well as girls. At cer-

tain seasons of the year he used to give the students rhubarb sauce every day for weeks together. That was thought to be just like Bangs, and I remember that one night the boys covered the front steps of the Seminary with pie-plant leaves. Mr. Bangs invented a coffee-pot, and that, too, seemed in character.

While I was staying at the Seminary when I was ill, I had got to think better of Mr. Bangs. As my freshman vacation approached, it occurred to me that it would be a good thing to travel about the country and sell Mr. Bangs' coffee-pot. My brother John was then in Galesburg, attending the preparatory school, and I decided to take him with me on this venture. He was staying with Professor Willard, and I remember that the Willards expressed their displeasure that my younger brother had been drawn into my restless and disintegrating orbit.

About the middle of June, John and I set off, headed toward Chicago. The coffee-pot was a very simple affair, so constructed that the coffee could be kept or boiled any length of time without losing its aroma. We carried with us a sample pot, with which we demonstrated. We took orders and then had the coffee-pots made up at the nearest hardware shop. I had a little metal die with which I hammered on each the word "Patented" before delivering them.

We sold a few coffee-pots between Galesburg and Chicago, and a few more in Valparaiso, where I was known, but on the whole the thing did not go very well. This was disappointing, as I had expected to make a great deal of money. We went from Valparaiso to Michigan City, Indiana, on the south shore of Lake Michigan in a very sandy country. The sand drifted like snow through the streets of the town, and this sand tract extended for some miles inland. Here the coffee-pot did not go at all.

My cousin Mr. Samuel N. Brengan, in a recent letter, throws some light on this early commercial venture.

". . . I afterwards met you in Tecumseh, Michigan, and recollect very well your visit there. Unfortunately I have not had an opportunity of meeting you since, and have often regretted that your circumstances never brought me into personal touch with you.

"Mother was much affected by the recital of your early struggles both in Ireland and this country. She was familiar with all the conditions and incidents you describe in the former place and could realize to the fullest the difficulties you and your mother were up against.

"She also remembers your visit to Tecumseh when we lived there, and often speaks of it. How you sold her a percolating coffee pot, and what splendid appetites you and Mr. Brady had for her cake and doughnuts."

And Mr. A. M. Turner, who wrote to me last December, further endorses Mr. Bangs' great invention:

"You may not recall the fact that you stopped at our house a few days in Crown Point while you were selling coffee pots, and you succeeded in disposing of one to my mother. I cannot say that the family regarded the investment thereafter as a good one, and for a long time the coffee pot stood around unused, a reminder of the incident."

In demonstrating the merits of Mr. Bangs' invention, however, I had learned to make excellent coffee. John and I took one of the town boys into partnership and opened a restaurant in an empty store building. I made the coffee, and the new boy's mother cooked a roast of beef for us. We sold a roast-beef sandwich and a cup of coffee for eight cents, and we called ourselves the "Enterprise Restaurant." The only trouble was that nobody wanted to buy sandwiches. In a town of about five thousand people everybody lived at home and went home for three meals a day. We ate more sandwiches than we sold, by a good many. After several dull days we had left just thirty-nine cents and our sample coffee-pot, and we felt that it was time to get out.

Where to go, was the next question. We had three uncles living in Tecumseh, Michigan—three of father's brothers who had come over from Ireland and established themselves there in the lumber district. We decided that we had better try to get to them and get work of some sort. But Tecumseh was about a hundred and fifty miles away, and thirty-nine cents would not take two boys very far on the railroad.

Finally we got on the train for New Buffalo, Michigan, eleven miles away. I have not the slightest idea what we expected to do there. We had not enough money to pay our fare, but we promised the conductor that if he would carry us through, we would make some money and pay him the rest of our fare. I suppose we must have been honest-looking boys, for he took us on through. He seemed surprised, however, when we afterward gave him the money.

We arrived at New Buffalo without a copper. It was a warm summer night, and we alternately sat on the board sidewalk, and walked up and down, talking to the night watchman, until morning. When it began to grow light we felt pretty hungry, so we struck off into the country to a near-by farm-house. Nobody was up there, so we went into the stable, cleaned it out, and began to split wood at the woodpile. When the farmer came out, we showed him what we had done and asked if he could give us some breakfast. He told us to come into the house and sit down until breakfast was ready.

On the sitting-room table were some books, among them a copy of Virgil. I sat down and began to read. When the farmer came in, he asked me why that book interested me, and I told him that I was a student at Knox College. He was very cordial, and said that he was a Knox College man himself. After breakfast he bought our sample coffee-pot for one dollar, and we went back to town.

In town we saw two men selling lampwicks and pins and cheap hosiery and handkerchiefs on the street. We bought a dollar's worth of their stock, and went about selling it from house to house until we had sold it for two dollars. Then we went back to the men and bought two dollars' worth of notions. This time they gave us the address of a firm in Chicago that made a business of supplying peddlers. We ordered five dollars' worth of goods to be sent us C. O. D., paid for them, and sold them.

As we went on and were more successful, we grew more ambitious and our orders were larger. In theory, we were still heading for Tecumseh, to reach our uncles; but now that we had found this new and diverting occupation, we were not in any pressing hurry to get there.

For boys there is always a fascination about selling things. Then, there was an element of chance about peddling that was very attractive. Every house we stopped at was a new adventure. It was very exciting to see how much we could sell.

When I was a little boy on the farm, I had always envied the peddlers who came along. Their life had seemed to me a free and easy one—always going on to some new place—and the goods they lifted out of their packs had always seemed more interesting and tempting than the goods one saw in the stores. It seemed a little as if the goods themselves might have had adventures.

When we reached Elkhart, Indiana, we found a package of twenty dollars' worth of goods waiting for us at the express office. When we had paid for them we had exactly one cent left. We traded off some of our goods for a night's lodging and breakfast, and left Elkhart at six o'clock the next morning with our packs on our backs. We were in great good spirits, and as we crossed the bridge over the St. Joseph River, going out of town, we flipped our remaining penny into the river for luck.

Our packs were pretty heavy that day—twenty dollars' worth of small notions made a considerable bulk—and we walked all day long, covering twenty-four miles and selling at most of the places where we stopped. By nightfall we reached the town of White Pigeon, pretty well done out. There we traded for our supper and looked about for a place to sleep. We had money now, of course, but it was our rule never to spend actual money when we could avoid it.

We usually got away from small towns at night and slept at farm-houses; for the country people were more ready to take socks and handkerchiefs and note-paper in exchange for a night's lodging than the town people were. But that night it seemed pretty late to start off into the country, so we thought we would go down to the depot and see if we could catch a ride out of town on a freight. We had had enough walking for that day, and we wanted to try some other method of getting over the country.

When we got to the depot, there stood a train

all ready for us, made up, with the engine attached. We selected a clean empty box-car that had been used for carrying lumber, and settled ourselves on the clean strips of bark that littered the floor, chuckling over our good luck. But presently, when the train started, my heart sank. We did not pull out with the proper energy; the engine puffed lazily, not as if she were getting down to business. My misgivings were not mistaken. The engine backed us out on a side-track, left us, and went puffing back.

There was nothing for it but to try a farm-house; so we struck off into the country. But it was getting late by this time—late for country people, anyhow—and we found all the houses dark. The farmers and their families were in bed. I wanted to pound on the door and waken some-body, but John was opposed to this. He begged me to try a haystack instead. We had slept in hay-stacks before and found them comfortable. We took to the fields, but we found the haystacks as inhospitable as the farm-houses. Every stack in that part of the country, apparently, was on stilts, built up two or three feet from the ground.

By this time we were so tired that our resource-fulness failed us; we had no power of invention left. We did the most obvious thing, which was to walk on all night. When we got into a little town next morning, we had been walking for twenty-four hours at a stretch, carrying our heavy packs, and had covered more than forty miles, not counting deflections from our course. That night we walked like the mechanical toys that are wound up with a key and sold on street corners, stiff-kneed, letting our bodies hang on our skeletons like clothes on a clothes-horse.

That was the most complete experience of bodily fatigue I have ever known. Years afterward I asked Stevenson how he knew so well the feelings of extreme fatigue which he describes in his hero in "Kidnapped." He laughed and said he had been through all that himself.

I have forgotten the name of the town, but we found a temperance hotel there, took a room, and went to bed at about six o'clock in the morning. We tumbled in pretty much any way, not even taking the trouble to open the windows or close the blinds. The room had probably not been aired for weeks. At ten o'clock we were awakened by the intolerable heat and closeness of the room. The sun was blazing in at the windows and shining in our faces. We were both very lame and dusty, our feet were terribly sore, and we had not had much of a rest, after all.

It was impossible to go to sleep again, so I got up and washed, and thought I would see if there was any business to be done in that town. My feet were so sore that I walked carefully and did not make much speed. I carried my big valise the whole length of the longest street in the town, and the only sale I was able to make was to a negro family among the poor scattered houses at the far end of the street. There I sold ten cents' worth. Staying in town always meant expense, so, tired though we were, that afternoon we tramped out into the country.

That penny we threw into the river for luck must have hit the water wrong, for things kept on going badly. We pushed ahead all that afternoon but at nightfall we were not able to make our usual comfortable arrangement of getting supper and a bed in exchange for some of our goods. On the contrary, we struck a very disagreeable farmer who made us pay twenty-five cents for a bed, and sleep two in a bed, at that. That was almost unheard of with us, to pay out real money for a bed—and in the country, too, where we had always been able to get along so easily.

The only time I ever resembled a financier was when I was a peddler; then I hated to part with real money just as much as a financier does.

Ordinarily, fifty cents' worth of goods would support one for twenty-four hours, that is, would give one a lodging and three meals. I seldom had to pay out currency, but lived on my pack as the camel does upon its hump.

On good days, when one made plenty of sales, peddling was very agreeable work indeed; one did not get tired or notice the distance one covered. There was something exciting about it. People in little towns and in the country were usually friendly and glad to see a couple of peddler boys come along; we created a distraction. But on bad days, when sales were poor, peddling was very discouraging work. The big black oilcloth valises in which we carried our goods grew very heavy, the roads seemed dusty and hot, and the houses far apart. The morning after we left the house of the disagreeable farmer, we had one of these bad days. We tramped on to Coldwater, Michigan. Accumulated discouragements told on John, and at Coldwater that day he struck, and said he wouldn't peddle another day, another mile—that a peddler's life was not the life for him.

After John announced his resolution, we took the train to Tecumseh, Michigan, where our three uncles were living. Two of them owned a sawmill, and worked at my father's trade, carpentering;

the other ran a grocery store. He hired me, and I worked in his store all summer as a clerk. I didn't like it half so well as peddling. Whenever I think of that store, I think of darkness and confinement, of being shut in a narrow, dusky room while there was sunlight outside. I plunged into that store every day as if I were going into prison.

While I was working in the store, my grandfather McClure died in Ireland, leaving all the grandchildren who were named after him (of whom I was one) ten pounds apiece. This helped me out of my immediate difficulties, and I went back to Valparaiso to see my mother, who had secured a country school for me a few miles north of Valparaiso.

She was bent upon my taking that school, and I had to admit that my peddling had not got me much ahead in funds for the winter's work at college. So that winter I stayed away from Knox and dropped behind a year. The school I taught was near my old friends; the work was pleasant of its kind, I suppose; and the people were certainly very kind. But there I registered my third and last failure at teaching a country school clear through to the end of the term. I stuck it out until spring. But I could never keep at any job in the spring; so, when the first mild days came, I bolted. I forget what excuse I made, or whether I made any; but I got me a pack and was off on the road again.

Dr. F. J. Scott, who has apparently been reading my autobiography in serial form, wrote me recently asking a pertinent question about a horse trade.

"I am anxious to get to the place where you spent a part of your summer vacation on my father's farm in Whitside Co. just five and a half miles from this town. I hope you will mention this trip and vacation in your story. Why not? Those were *good old days*.

"Well do I remember how you and my brother H. B., who graduated at Knox with you, pitched hay in the field and at the big red barn. Also I remember how you traded the bay mare you were driving on your wagon to my brother Ed for a big, rangy grey gelding. . . . I am anxious for the story."

The story is this.

It distressed my mother to see how tired and foot-sore I would return from these peddling tramps, so she bought me a wagon with an oilcloth top, like a grocer's delivery wagon, and a little brown horse. This was a great improvement over peddling on foot. I set off on a long trip with a considerable stock of goods. I particularly liked my little mare. She was great company on a long drive, a most companionable and willing and amiable little beast. After a time I came to a town where Scott, one of my old room-mates at Knox, lived. He asked me to drive round to his house, and introduced me to his people. They all came out and looked my outfit over, remarking that it was a pity that my horse had a contraction of the hoofs that would soon make her useless for the road. I was naturally concerned about this. They said they had a white horse, much larger and stronger than mine, that would serve my purpose better, and they soon persuaded me to trade. I drove out of town with this big white horse, which was much older than my mare, and of no class. I had not driven very far out of town before it occurred to me that, in persuading me to trade, my friends had not altogether had my interests at heart. I never liked that white horse, and was always a little ashamed of him, besides regretting my brown mare.

It was early in May, 1879, when I left Valparaiso, Indiana, and started off across Illinois, headed for Galesburg. My direction was determined by a rumor that had reached me, to the effect that Miss Hurd either had returned or was to return to Galesburg. It had been two years since I had either seen her or heard from her. If I had been very hopeful of an interview with her, there would have been ways of getting there, certainly. But, in a way, youth is always hopeful, and I naturally went in that direction.

When I started for Galesburg, I took my brother Tom with me part of the way. Business was good, and I usually made from two to two and a half dollars a day above our expenses.

The distance from Valparaiso to Galesburg, by wagon road, is something over two hundred miles. I reached Galesburg in the latter part of May, having been about two weeks on the way. I went almost at once to Professor Hurd's house, for as soon as I reached town I had assured myself that Miss Hurd had really returned to Galesburg. Mrs. Hurd, Harriet's mother, met me at the door, and told me that Harriet was at home but did not wish to see me again. This seemed final enough. I went away, and sent back to Miss Hurd the photograph of herself she had given me, and some other little keepsakes. She sent back my remembrances in like manner.

Since I could not see Miss Hurd, there was not much point in staying in Galesburg any longer. I started back across Illinois again, toward Valparaiso. I have always remembered that trip for its singular beauty. It was in haying season, and I had glorious moonlight most of the way across the State. The weather was perfect haying weather, mild and warm, with no rain at all. I slept out of doors every night of the way. The hay had not been stacked yet, and was drying in little cocks which dotted the fields. I used to take a few armfuls of this fresh hay, carry it to the edge of the field near the road, spread my quilts upon it, and go to sleep beside the wagon, with the horse picketed near by. It was, of course, a rolling prairie country, with soft dirt roads and rail fences—wire fences had not then come into use—and numerous walnut and hickory groves. I usually ate out of doors, too. I used often to buy a good steak in town, some potatoes, and canned peaches, perhaps, and then stop and build a fire in a grove and cook my steak on a green stick. I afterward recounted those peddling experiences very fully to Stevenson, and he attributed some of them to Jim Pinkerton in "The Wrecker."

That summer I crossed Illinois three times in my wagon. Soon after I returned to Valparaiso after my first round trip, I started back toward Galesburg again, and this time I took my mother with me. I had friends all along the road by this time, and they received my mother and me with the greatest friendliness and entertained us like visitors. My mother always had 'the spare room and the best the house afforded. We always spent the night at a farm-house or in a village, but our dinner we usually cooked and ate in the open, in some attractive spot along the road. My mother had a roving disposition like my own, and she enjoyed that trip immensely. She was pleased by the cordiality of the people along the way.

When we got to Galesburg, I remained there and went on with my work at Knox College. That sophomore year was easier in every way than the preceding ones had been, and, like happy nations, it had no history. Whenever I ran short of funds, I shouldered my pack and went away into the country for a few days, and returned with money enough to go on for a while. I had at last found a vocation exactly suited to my nature and to my needs, that could be taken up and dropped again at will: a means of making money that was easy, pleasant, nomadic, and especially adapted to broken time.

Before my sophomore year was over, a manual of shorthand came into my possession, and I decided to learn shorthand. As soon as the term closed, I went to Chicago and entered a business college where shorthand was taught. There were two shorthand systems in vogue then, the Munson system and that devised by Ben Pitman. I lived in a boarding-house on Michigan Avenue, and, either at the boarding-house or at the business college, I met a young fellow, about my own age, who had been in the Pinkerton detective service, but who was now studying shorthand. We became good friends, and I soon infected him with the peddling fever. I was hungering for the open fields again, and I persuaded him that we could take a stock of goods out into the country, sell enough to supply our immediate necessities, and teach each other shorthand as we wandered along. He agreed that this would be much better than a hot summer in Chicago. I had money enough to buy a stock—he may have put in some money, too; I do not remember—and we set off on the road again.

I remember that summer as one of the happiest of my life; a green summer, with delightful companionship and no cares. We peddled only incidentally. Our main business was practising shorthand.

We spent about six weeks wandering through a most beautiful country—the northern part of Indiana, immediately south of Lake Michigan. We lived in the open, in the woods and groves, near the little towns in which we peddled and traded and bought our food. When we tired of one neighborhood, we would board a convenient freight-car and go on. We used to lie on the grass in a good green wood all day long, giving each other dictation.

I had even forgotten my comrade's name, but had so often wished that I could hear from him again that I hoped he might chance to read this narrative and make himself known to me, a wish which was subsequently realized in a roundabout way. The fact that he had never, to my memory, told me anything about his past life or about his family made the task of looking him up seem impossible at the time I prepared this autobiography. He was very uncommunicative, and yet perfectly frank and open. I think he must have made a good detective. I do remember distinctly that, in that whole summer that we spent together, there was no friction or misunderstanding of any kind. He had none of the petty selfishness that spoils everything when two people travel together. He never grumbled at anything, or wished that we had done something different. He took good and bad luck with the same equanimity. He had a curious easiness of mind and body, was exceptionally well poised and well muscled, and an expert boxer. We frequently went into saloons of a Saturday night to sell goods, often in the mining regions where there was a rough crowd assembled, but nobody ever took any liberties with that young fellow. He was the sort of boy who could elbow his way through a quarrelsome crowd without giving offense and without losing his coolness. I have no recollection of where or how we parted. Boys take such friendships lightly.

Imagine my pleasure, then, upon receiving, at the time this narrative appeared in magazine form, the following clue:

"ITHACA, N. Y., DEC. 23, 1913

"S. S. McClure

"Dear Sir:

"I have been much interested in your life history running in your magazine, and today I learned who was your companion in the summer trip, with whom you worked out the shorthand methods. He lives in Ithaca, and in conversation with him this evening I learned from him that a friend of his, having heard him speak of having been associated with a McClure in his youth, had told him of the articles in the magazine. I hunted up the back numbers and gave them to him, relating some of the escapades which he remembered having heard you mention and others in which he was your comrade; also he spoke of some you write of. You mention what is still characteristic of him, his reserve; and fearing he will not write you, I am writing this. His name is Tichenor, which name I hope you will recall. I trust you will hear from him direct.

"Among other incidents Mr. Tichenor mentioned having been brought up with you before a justice of the peace and that you, knowing the magistrate's daughter, wrote a note to her which was the means of your pardon for the offence. (I forget what he said it was.)

"(Signed) D. Mitchell,
"204 Stewart Ave.,
Ithaca, N. Y."

Apparently Mr. Mitchell extended his good services by making my whereabouts known to Mr. Tichenor, for the latter wrote me within a few days:

"ITHACA, N. Y., DEC. 31, 1913
"Dear Friend Sam:

"Doubtless after all these intervening years you will be surprised to receive a communication from me. Therefore will explain.

"On Sunday last, a friend called at my house, saying that he believed he had something that would be of interest to me. He then produced the January, 1914, copy of McClure's Magazine, and read the part in your biographical sketch, relating to incidents which I at once recognized as having taken part in.

"You cannot imagine what a feeling of pleasure passed through my mind when I realized that you had succeeded in your business under such difficulties.

"This friend had heard me speak of you on several occasions. I first learned of your connection with the magazine business some years ago, when I saw a periodical which contained several cuts of prominent magazine publishers, and I at once recognized your picture. That brought to my mind very vividly the time we had spent together, walking, running, and navigating in other ways through Indiana.

"My identification card is inclosed—this postal of the 80's. You will observe that I have taken good care of it and consider it now as a souvenir.

"Thanking you for the kindly mention which you made of me in your January issue, and hoping that this letter may be answered and our friendship of former years be renewed, I will now close by wishing you a Happy and Prosperous New Year.

"Your friend,

(Signed) Geo. E. Tichenor."

The "identification card" mentioned is reproduced herewith. The mysterious dots and dashes go to show how enthusiastically we carried on our shorthand practice in those days, reducing our let-

Galesburg - Tuesday —

$50⁰⁰ that cost $125⁰⁰.
If you can get one at a good bargain. L. Write
Yours truly. as

ters to cipher messages which often looked more important than they were.

In a subsequent letter he recalls a day which contained adventures a little above the average.

"I presume you remember our being "pulled" by a constable for selling goods without a license, in Michigan City; and when taken before the magistrate you discovered at once that he (the M.) had a daughter with whom you were acquainted. You immediately wrote said daughter of our plight, and I believe she sent back word to go easy on us; but the court took all but 50 cents of our cash—about $7—and when night came we began to look about for a resting place. I remember we went down under that big sand hill (called Hoorer's Slide, I believe), but a short distance from the lake, and there we dug a hole and stuck up some pieces of wood we found along the shore to shield us from the strong lake wind. There we spent the night and next morning we pulled out via a "convenient freight train." Where we landed I cannot just now recall, but do remember being chased by some of the trainmen. They were not quite swift enough for us."

In parting from this young girl who had tried to help us, I gave her a photograph-frame as a souvenir. In later years as a reader of *McClure's Magazine* she remembered her connection with this incident of the editor's youth, wrote me recalling these circumstances, and returned to me as a reminder the little gift of long ago. Then a few years later I received from her family the announcement of her death.

The next summer I had an equally delightful companion in Albert Brady; but that was a friendship which was to last and to be of great importance to both of us. Albert later assisted Mr. Phillips and me in founding *McClure's Magazine,* and became Advertising Manager. He was associated with me in that capacity until his death in Rome in 1900.

I well remember Albert as he looked when he

first came to Knox, in my sophomore year. He was a slim youth, with dark eyes and a thoughtful, candid expression. I think he must have grown several inches during his first year at college; indeed, it seems to me that he grew that much within a month or two. His trousers were always too short for him that first year. Our friendship grew out of our mutual interest in mathematics. Albert used to come to my room, and we would often work all night over a problem. There were then certain historical "test problems" that were given out to the classes year after year, and upon which we were all expected to fail. Once Albert and I worked at such a problem for eighteen hours at a sitting— from six o'clock Saturday night until Sunday noon.

Albert lived at a good boarding-house, and his mother used to send him boxes of supplies which were very useful. I remember that I once ate a whole roast chicken in his room. He came to room with me before the year was over, and we roomed together most of the time during my last three years in college. Albert, too, was a fellow who could accept any little miscarriage of one's plans without any squealing. During the first winter that we roomed together he got a heavy cold and was confined to his bed for several days. I decided that what he needed was an outing—and I knew I needed one. We each took a valise full of goods and went down to the C., B. & Q. station, found a brakeman whom we knew, and arranged to beat our way on a freight train to a crossing where the Rock Island tracks ran under those of the Q.

It was a very cold winter night. We first got into a car of shelled corn. I thought this was lucky enough. I had ridden in cars of shelled corn and oats in summer, and had always found them reservoirs of heat; so I thought we would have a very comfortable passage. But we found the corn almost as cold as pulverized ice. It extracted the heat from our bodies in place of giving us heat. As soon as we could, we changed for an open cattle-car. As Albert had got thoroughly chilled, I took off his shoes and rubbed his feet, working over him for some time. When we reached the crossing, we got out and waited for the train coming along the Rock Island tracks. Early in the morning we arrived in La Salle. Albert spent the day in bed, and I crossed over the river to a little settlement I had often visited, and spent the day peddling. I sold five dollars' worth. The next day was Sunday, and we visited the family of one of our classmates. Sunday night we returned to Galesburg in the same way we had left it. Albert was, on the whole, a good deal better than when we set out, and I had made some money.

Albert Brady and I spent the summer of our junior year traveling around the Great Lakes, selling microscopes. It came about quite by chance. One spring day I was walking down a street in Galesburg, when I saw a man on the street corner selling small microscopes for a dollar apiece. I went up to him, and got into conversation with him. I asked him what the microscopes cost him wholesale, and he told me three dollars a dozen. This seemed to offer opportunities. I talked it over with Albert, and he agreed to go in with me. When the term was over, we went to his home in Davenport, Iowa, from which point we were to set out. Albert's father published a newspaper in Davenport, and he got Albert a pass to St. Paul. I got a deck passage on a Mississippi steamer, the *Gem City*, and spent two nights lying across three deck-chairs. I had put all my money into microscopes, so I subsisted on a bag of crackers I had brought along. Albert and I met unexpectedly in the corridor of a hotel in St. Paul. The next day Albert went to Minneapolis to sell his microscopes, while I remained in St. Paul to sell mine. I also worked in Stillwater, where I one day sold ten dollars' worth.

Our methods of selling were simple. We got a store box, stood it on end on a street corner, spread out our magnifying-glasses, and waited for bites. If any one came up and glanced curiously at our stock, we invited him to take a look. We kept a few bits of quartz which looked very pretty under the glass, some insect wings, flowers, etc. By letting a weed or a flower remain in a glass of water for a day or two we could produce a mass of amœbæ, which our customers used to examine under the glass with great interest. I remember that a great many of them used to say that those little animals were the life of the water—that if they were not there human beings would not get any nourishment from the water they drank.

After we got tired of Minneapolis and St. Paul, Albert and I moved on to Brainerd and Duluth. In these places the authorities demanded a license sufficiently large to prevent any possibility of making a profit. Our chief problem, therefore, was to evade this license. In Duluth we rented a vacant lot for fifty cents, set up our dry-goods box, and began to sell goods. A policeman came along and asked to see our license; but we explained to him that we were selling goods on our own rented property, and if we were subject to taxation we were ready to pay it at the end of the year. He took us before the city authorities; but they found our position unassailable and did not interfere with us further. A few days later we went on to Cleveland by steamer, and from there worked our way westward again to Michigan City, Chicago, Davenport, and Galesburg. When we got back to college, we had traveled upward of three thousand miles, had made a little money, and were better friends than ever. Then we began upon our senior work at Knox.

Besides building up my health and enabling me to go to school, the peddling experiences of those three summers had given me a very close acquaintance with the people of the small towns and the farming communities, the people who afterward bought *McClure's Magazine.* I had stayed all night at the homes of many of these people, and had heard all about their business affairs. In many of the little towns I was known by name in every house in the town. I had found out that, for the most part, all these people were interested in exactly the same things, or the same kind of thing, that interested me. Years later, when I came to edit a popular magazine, I could never believe in that distinction made by some editors that "this or that was very good, but it wouldn't interest the people of the Middle West, or the people in the little towns." My experience had taught me that the people in the little towns were interested in whatever was interesting—that they were just like the people in New York or Boston. I felt myself to be a fairly representative Middle-Westerner. I bought and printed what interested me, and it usually seemed to interest the other Middle-Westerners.

By losing a year at Knox the winter I stayed out to teach school, I graduated with the class of '82, and I have always considered this fortunate. The class of '82 left a mark in Knox College, a reputation for mental initiative and intellectual turbulence. The boys of that class were somewhat difficult to manage because they were so active, adopted ideas, and took sides very vehemently. The boys were not the kind of fellows who express themselves in practical jokes and gaucheries, such as putting a cow in the chapel. When they made a disturbance, it was always because of some new idea they had got hold of, or that had got hold of them.

We were not a lawless class, but we did not accept traditions. We departed from some of the established customs. We went at things fresh, and did not do certain things simply because other seniors had done them. Like the Athenians, we were always discussing. Some of the professors have told me since that there never was such a class for talking, and that whenever they opened a window they could hear some of us arguing on the campus. Among the boys of this class were some very strong personalities, notably Robert Mather, John Phillips, and Albert Brady. These boys were all singularly mature for their age, forceful and well balanced even as lads.

John S. Phillips, who afterward assisted me to found *McClure's Magazine*, and who is now editor of the *American Magazine*, was a Galesburg boy, and had entered Knox College the year I was out teaching school. He was recognized as a boy of unusual ability. Phillips and Brady and I generally worked together in class fights and college affairs.

Robert Mather later became president of the Rock Island Railway Company, and at the time of his death in the fall of 1911 he was chairman of the Westinghouse Electrical Companies. At the time he attended Knox College, his father was working in the Q. shops in Galesburg as a mechanic. Robert worked there in a clerical capacity and made his own expenses. He was a firm, cool-headed boy, who always seemed to know exactly where he was going and what he was going to do. He struck one at once as mature and resourceful, and thoroughly the

(1) JOHN S. PHILLIPS, NOW EDITOR OF THE "AMERICAN MAGAZINE"
(2) ROBERT MATHER   (3) ALBERT BRADY

KNOX COLLEGE WITH GLIMPSE OF "WEST BRICKS," WHERE S. S. MC CLURE ROOMED

master of himself. There was plenty of fun in him and he was companionable. He took an active part in college politics, and felt very strongly about student matters that he had become interested in. Mather thought he had been unfairly treated in an essay contest in his sophomore year, and the vigor with which he retaliated resulted in a class fight such as had never been seen at Knox before, and involved the whole college.

One of the results of this fight was that, early in their senior year, Mather and his faction secured control of the *Knox College Student*. The paper had never belonged to any one; the editors were not regularly elected, but the senior class usually conducted the paper in some informal manner. This time, however, Mather and his supporters had not consulted the rest of the class at all, but had simply taken possession. Very soon after they got control, the office of the paper was entered one night and the subscription list and the books were removed. To this day I do not know who took them, nor did I at the time imagine that it had been done for our benefit. But the books soon came into our hands, and Albert Brady, John Phillips, a classmate named Evans, and I took hold of the *Knox Student* and had it legally incorporated in Springfield.

There were twenty-six of us in the group that opposed Mather, and we each held two shares of stock in the paper. I was made Editor in Chief, Phillips Literary Editor, and Albert Brady Business Manager. Albert at once had some contract blanks printed, and went around to the business men of Galesburg and got them to sign up for a year's advertising. Meanwhile, because of our high-handedness, public sympathy in the college had swung the other way, and when Mather came out with a new publication, the *Coup d'Etat*, the lower classmen were all with him, and his new paper really was more representative of the student body than was the *Knox Student*. When Mather's people went about to get advertising for the new paper, however, they found that all the merchants had signed contracts with us and they refused to give out any more advertising to college publications.

We put out a very good college paper. John Phillips was easily the best read student in the college, a boy with a great natural aptitude for letters; and Albert Brady showed then the same unusual business ability that he afterward showed as Business Manager of *McClure's Magazine*. It was curious how, after we left college, the three of us held together. It does not often happen that three boys, united in a college enterprise, keep in touch with one another and a few years after their graduation form a business partnership that lasts through a large part of their lives. Robert Mather, too, during the latter years of his life was associated with our enterprises, and at the time of his death was vice-president of the board of directors of the S. S. McClure Company.

In editing the *Knox Student* I followed exactly the same principles of editing that I afterward followed in editing *McClure's Magazine*. Whatever I know about editing I knew in the beginning. We had, after the manner of college papers, a long staff of contributing editors, an Exchange Editor, a Society Editor, etc. I remember that at first some of them were very indignant at the way in which I cut and modified their copy. There was especial indignation because I cut all such items as: "Charley Brown was seen walking across the campus with a vision in white last Friday afternoon. What about it, Charley?" Phillips and I had undertaken to make the paper lively and interesting, and we didn't consider this form of humor either one or the other.

I had never in any way distinguished myself in my English classes, and some of our contributors who had written prize essays were naturally indignant at the liberties I took in cutting and condensing their copy. Some of the disgruntled boys had a meeting of the stockholders called, at which they intended to make a motion to depose me. They introduced some minor motion first to test the strength of their following, and when Albert Brady got up and announced that he had been empowered to vote twenty-six proxies, the meeting went no further.

In looking over the exchanges from other colleges, one day, it occurred to me that it would be a good thing to write a history of the college papers of Western Colleges. I talked this over with Mr. Phillips, and he seemed to think it would be interesting. I suppose we were somewhat influenced by a desire to set forth modestly our own triumphs in college journalism. I corresponded with a number of colleges, and got up and printed a pamphlet which I called "The History of Western College Journalism." After the book was written, I went to the public library and looked over the advertising in all the big magazines. I made a note of such houses as I thought might advertise with profit in college publications, wrote to them, and got advertising enough to make a small sum of money on my pamphlet. This was the first touch of any kind that I had ever had with the advertising department of big business concerns. One of these advertisements, the one I secured from the Pope Manufacturing

Company, was to have a very important influence on my future.

On September 15 of my senior year I saw Harriet Hurd for the first time in nearly five years. I was walking through the public park adjoining the college campus, when I saw her walking some distance ahead of me. I overtook her and after some hesitation spoke to her, saying that I was afraid that she was under some misapprehension about me. She turned in a pleasant, friendly way, as if she had seen me only the day before, and said that she did not feel that there was any misunderstanding, and that she felt that things had never changed between us. I talked with her for a moment then, and arranged to see her that evening. I called accordingly, and I remember that evening as distinctly the happiest of my life. We met again as if we had not been separated for nearly five years, with complete sympathy and understanding. I stayed until the cuckoo clock chirped ten—which was the latest hour that any boy could, on any pretext, stay in Professor Hurd's house.

Just at this time the young Professor of English Literature at Knox College, Melville B. Anderson, was a most kind and useful friend to us. He organized a class for the study of Anglo-Saxon, to which Miss Hurd and I were both bidden, and then and always has been our sympathizer. Years later Mrs. McClure and I visited Professor and Mrs. Anderson at Palo Alto, California, where he was Professor of English Literature at Leland Stanford University, and in a letter written after this visit he says—

"Don't forget to give our (and *my*) love to Harriet. Remember, you and she, that, or thank the Anglo-Saxon class, the cup might have slipped from the parched lip. And, moreover, the good account I gave of you when asked! So I claim a place in that "very tender history."

After that I saw Miss Hurd nearly every day until she left Galesburg in March. Her father was anxious to have her go away, chiefly because I was there. She had an opportunity to teach in the University of Nebraska, at Lincoln, and another position was offered her at the Abbot Academy, in Andover, Massachusetts. Professor Hurd thought it would be too easy for a young man just out of college to locate in Lincoln, but that in Andover a boy from the West would have a pretty hard time to get along; so he insisted that Harriet should go to Andover. After she went to Andover in the spring, Miss Hurd and I corresponded, and she gave me permission to visit her in the summer, when she would be staying with friends near Utica, New York.

My commencement oration was on "Enthusiasm,"

and it lasted exactly five minutes. It stated about as much as I have ever had to say on that subject: that the men who start the great new movements in the world are enthusiasts whose eyes are fixed upon the end they wish to bring about—that to them the future becomes present. It was when they believed in what seemed impossible that the Abolitionists did most good, that they created the sentiment which finally did accomplish the impossible. The enthusiast, I argued, must always be considered impractical, because he ignores those difficulties of execution which make most men conservative; and his impracticality is his strength. It is not the critical, judicial type of mind, but the Garibaldi type of mind, that generates the great popular ideas by which humanity rights itself.

When I wrote my oration I had one clear picture in mind, though I did not use this figure at all in the oration. It was that of a man out in the open on a dark night, and before him, on a hilltop, a light shining. Between this man and that light there were woods and brambles and sloughs and marshes and deep rivers. But the man was so unconscious of all this that it seemed to him he could already put out his hand and touch the light. This kind of man, I felt, would in some fashion get what he started out for.

My graduation was one of the greatest disappointments I have ever been through. I had done well enough in my studies, and graduated third in a class of thirty—Mather was first, and Nils Anderson, a Swede, second. But I had expected to be a very different fellow when I got through college from the fellow I had always been. When I found that I was still just the same boy, a feeling of discouragement weighed me down. I had looked forward for eight years to graduating, and I had always thought that when I graduated I would be tall, that I would know a great deal, and that I would have all the plans made for my life. Here I was, no taller, no wiser, and with no plans at all. The future was an absolute blank ahead of me. I could not see a step in advance. I talked with other boys, and found that most of them had arranged for the immediate future. One classmate was going into his father's law office; another was going to enter his uncle's store; several were going to teach in high schools or small colleges, etc. As I talked things over with them, it occurred to me that they were tying themselves up pretty early, and that, though it was uncomfortable not to have any plans, I did not want to tie myself up, as they were doing. I figured that when so many boys from so many colleges were going into regular lines of work that year, there might be room for one irregular—that it couldn't hurt anybody but myself if I took a plunge into space.

In the week of my commencement Miss Hurd's letters ceased coming. I wrote repeatedly, but could not get a reply from her. She had been, when I last heard from her, with her friends near Utica. There was evidently some misunderstanding. I waited about Galesburg for several days after commencement, but no letter came from Miss Hurd. One night, when John Phillips and I were sitting on the steps of the High School building, I talked the situation over with him, and he agreed with me that I had better go East and find out what was the trouble.

The next day I packed my valise. Besides my clothes, I put in a small stock of notions. Peddling had become second nature to me by this time. I still had some money I had made on my "History of Western College Journalism," but that would not last long, and I thought that if I failed to find work in the East I could fall back on my pack temporarily.

CHAPTER V

When I left Galesburg at the end of June, 1882, and started for Utica, New York, to find Miss Hurd, I was really leaving the West for good, but I did not know it then. I left very casually, without saying good-by to anyone, thinking that I would be back in a few weeks, perhaps. Or perhaps I did not really think about it at all. I simply got on the train for Chicago. One seldom realizes the critical moves in one's life until long afterward. And, though I lived so much in the future, I never looked ahead and planned; I finished one thing and did the next. The train on which I left Galesburg was headed straight for Life and Work and the Future; but I had no realization of this then.

I arrived at Utica, New York, June 30, 1882, early

in the morning. I caught the first train out for Marcy, where Miss Hurd was visiting her friend Miss Potter, an old schoolmate at Berthier-en-Haut. When I reached the house I was met by Miss Potter, who told me that Miss Hurd would prefer not to see me. I urged my case, however, until Miss Hurd consented to see me. My interview with Miss Hurd was almost too painful to describe here, and more than justified the fears that the ceasing of her letters had aroused in me. When I left her, I carried away the conviction that she had absolutely ceased to care for me—that I in every way displeased her and fell short of her expectations.

This dismissal I accepted as final. I walked back to the station at Marcy, and found that there would be no train for Utica for some time; so I walked on along the railroad tracks to Utica. Once, when I was walking along at the bottom of a cut, I heard a train coming behind me; for a moment I thought that it was not worth while to get out of the way.

When I reached Utica, I went to the station-master and asked him how soon there would be another train out. "Half an hour," he replied. I asked him where it went. He answered, "To Boston." So I asked him to give me a ticket to Boston. I had never in my life thought of going to Boston before, and I had no reason for going there now. I was merely going wherever the next train went, and as far as it went. Then I looked about for my valise, which contained all the clothing I had brought, as well as my stock of peddler's supplies. It was nowhere to be found, so I boarded the Boston train and went on without it.

I reached Boston late that night, and got out at the South Station in the midst of a terrible thunderstorm. I knew no one in Boston except Miss Malvina Bennett (now Professor of Elocution at Wellesley), who had taught elocution at Knox. She lived in Somerville, and I immediately set out for Somerville. If I had had my wits about me, I should not, of course, have started for anybody's house at that hour of the night. The trip to Somerville took more than an hour, and I had to change cars several times on the way. When I got to Miss Bennett's house, I found it open, and the members of the household, some of them at least, were up and dressed, on account of the serious illness of Miss Bennett's mother. I was taken in and made welcome, and for several days Miss Bennett and her family did all they could to make me comfortable and to help me to get myself established in some way. I remained with the Bennetts Saturday and Sunday. I had only six dollars, and this hospitality was of the utmost importance to me.

My first application for a job in Boston was made in accordance with an idea of my own.

Every boy in the West knew the Pope Manufacturing Company and the Columbia bicycle—the high, old-fashioned wheel which was then the only kind in general use. When I published my "History of Western College Journalism" the Pope Company had given me an advertisement, and that seemed to me a kind of "connection." I had always noticed the Pope advertisements everywhere. Everything about that company seemed to me progressive. As I learned afterward, it was a maxim of Colonel Pope's that " some advertising was better than others, but all advertising was good."

Monday the 3d of July was one of those clear, fresh days very common in Boston, where even in summer the air often has a peculiar flavor of the sea. I took the street car in from Somerville, and got off at Scollay Square. From there I walked a considerable distance up Washington Street to the offices of the Pope Manufacturing Company at 597, near where Washington crosses Bolyston. I walked into the general office and said I wanted to see the president of the company.

"Colonel Pope?" inquired the clerk.

I answered: "Yes, Colonel Pope."

I was taken to Colonel A. A. Pope, who was then

an alert, progressive man of thirty-nine. He had been an officer in the Civil War when a very young man, and after he entered business had, within a few years, made a very considerable fortune in manufacturing leather findings. Some years before this a Frenchman named Pierre Lallemont had taken out a patent for wheels driven by pedals attached to the axle—the basic patent of the bicycle. Colonel Pope saw the possibilities of this patent, and bought it. Though his patent right was continually being contested, and he had constantly to employ several patent lawyers to protect it, he held it until it expired, and all other bicycle manufacturers had to pay Colonel Pope a tax of ten dollars on every wheel they manufactured.

I told Colonel Pope, by way of introduction, that he had once given me an "ad" for a little book I had published. He said that he was sorry, but they were not giving out any more advertising that season. I replied respectfully that I didn't want any more advertising; that I had been a college editor, and now I was out of college and out of a job. What I wanted was work, and I wanted it very badly.

He again said he was sorry, but they were laying off hands. I still hung on. It seemed to me that everything would be all up with me if I had to go out of that room without a job. I had to have a job.

I asked him if there wasn't anything at all that I could do. My earnestness made him look at me sharply.

"Willing to wash windows and scrub floors?" he asked.

I told him that I was, and he turned to one of his clerks. "Has Wilmot got anybody yet to help him in the downtown rink?" he asked.

The clerk said he thought not.

"Very well," said Colonel Pope. "You can go to the rink and help Wilmot out for to-morrow."

The next day was the Fourth of July, and an extra man would be needed for that day.

I went to the bicycle rink on Huntington Avenue, and found that what Wilmot wanted was a man to teach beginners to ride. Now, I had never been on a bicycle in my life, nor even been very close to one; but I was in the predicament of the dog that had to climb a tree. In a couple of hours I had learned to ride a wheel myself and was teaching other people.

Next day Mr. Wilmot paid me a dollar. He did not say anything about my coming back the next morning; but I came, and went to work, very much afraid I would be told that I wasn't needed. After that Mr. Wilmot did not exactly engage me, but he forgot to discharge me, and I came back every day and went to work. I kept myself inconspicuous and worked diligently. At the end of the week Colonel Pope sent for me and placed me in charge of the uptown rink, over the general offices of the Pope Company on Washington Street.

Colonel Pope was a man who watched his workmen. I had not been mistaken when I felt that a young man would have a chance with him. He used often to say that "water would find its level," and he kept an eye on us. One day he called me into his office and asked me if I could edit a magazine.

"Yes, sir," I replied quickly. I remember it flashed through my mind that I could do anything I was put at just then—that if I were required to run an ocean steamer I could somehow manage to do it: I could learn to do it as I went along. I answered as quickly as I could get the words out of my mouth, afraid that Colonel Pope would change his mind before I could get them out. Then I added: "I could edit a monthly; I hardly think I could manage a weekly."

Then he told me that they were about to start a magazine, to be called the *Wheelman*, devoted to bicycling. I sent to Galesburg and got a file of the college paper I had edited, to show him what I could do in that line. When I was in college I had never read magazines. They were too expensive to buy.

It had always seemed remarkable to me that a man could ever feel rich enough to pay thirty-five cents for a magazine.

After I began to know John Phillips, in my junior year, and began to go to his house, I found magazines there. I remember one night taking up a copy of the *Century Magazine* and beginning the new serial, which happened to be "A Modern Instance," by Mr. Howells. That was the first serial I had ever read, and I followed it to the end with intense interest. In doing so I became fairly well acquainted with the *Century Magazine.*

When Colonel Pope was planning the first number of the magazine he was going to publish, I remembered having read an article on bicycling in the *Century*, called "A Wheel Around the Hub," which I thought would make an excellent article to open the first number of the *Wheelman*. I told Colonel Pope about it, and he sent me over to New York to buy the plates of the article and the right to republish it. I bought the plates for three hundred dollars, and took them back to Boston. When the question of the make-up and typography of the *Wheelman* arose, here I had the first article of the opening number in one kind of type; it would certainly be absurd to have the rest of the magazine in another. Since the *Century* was notably the best

American magazine typographically, I did not see why we should not adopt the *Century* idea of make-up throughout. So, when the first number of the *Wheelman* appeared, it looked exactly like the *Century*—somewhat to the astonishment of the publishers of the latter magazine, who had not intended to sell me their idea of make-up along with the plates of the article on bicycling.

As soon as plans for the *Wheelman* were fairly under way, it became clear that we would need a couple more men. I talked to Colonel Pope about John Phillips and my own brother John, and he told me to go ahead and send for them. The boys came on from Galesburg, and in a few weeks the three of us were established in offices at 608 Washington Street, near Colonel Pope's own offices.

The first number of the *Wheelman* came out in August, 1882, within two months after I left college, and, quite by accident, I was the editor of it. I had never expected to be an editor, or planned to be one; but now that I found myself one, I was not surprised. Before I knew it I had grown up, acquired responsibilities.

Up to this time I had always lived in the future and felt that I was simply getting ready for something. Now I began to live in the present. I had always regarded my occupations in college as temporary, and when I finished college I had not allowed myself to fall back on any of those temporary means of support in which boys take shelter while they look around. I felt now that I had managed to attach myself to something vital, where there was every possibility of development. I was in the big game, in the real business of the world; and I began to live in the present.

Colonel Pope's office, 597 Washington Street, was set back a little from the street; when you mounted the steps to enter the front door, you could not see the street down which you had come. It was just at that crook in the street that I said good-by to my youth. When I have passed that place in later years, I have fairly seen him standing there— a thin boy, with a face somewhat worn from loneliness and wanting things he couldn't get, a little hurt at being left so unceremoniously. When I went up the steps, he stopped outside; and it now seems to me that I stopped on the steps and looked at him, and that when he looked at me I turned and never spoke to him and went into the building. I came out with a job, but I never saw him again, and now I have no sense of identity with that boy; he was simply one boy whom I knew better than other boys. He had lived intensely in the future and had wanted a great many things. It tires me, even now, to remember how many things he had wanted. He had always lived in the country, and was an idealist to such an extent that he thought the world was peopled exclusively by idealists. But I went into business and he went back to the woods.

The *Wheelman*, when it appeared, as I have said, looked like a thinner *Century*. It had eighty pages of text and as many pages of advertisements as we could get. It was illustrated with wood engravings —that was before the days of half-tones—and sold for twenty cents a copy. We paid for contributions, but our contributors were oftener professional men—doctors, lawyers, ministers—than journalists or professional writers.

Bicycling was the first out-of-door sport that became generally popular in America; tennis and golf came later. Town men, who followed sedentary occupations, discovered the country on the bicycle. These enthusiasts sent us articles on everything that had to do with bicycling. Many of the most entertaining were accounts of long trips made through interesting parts of the country, and illustrated with photographs. We had a department devoted to bicycle clubs, and published accounts of meets and races. I spent a good part of my time traveling about to attend these meets and tournaments and

COLONEL ALBERT A. POPE

MRS. HARRIET PRESCOTT SPOFFORD

getting contributions from enthusiastic wheelmen. Mr. Phillips had general charge of the office.

One of the pleasantest trips I made in connection with my work on the *Wheelman* was to the home of Harriet Prescott Spofford, at Deer Island, just outside Newburyport. Mrs. Spofford's island was —and is still— all her own, beautifully situated in the middle of the Merrimac River. I rode down from Boston one Sunday to see whether I could persuade her to do some writing for the *Wheelman.* Mrs. Spofford was a woman of singular charm, tall, slender, with a beautifully shaped face and delicate coloring. I knew her stories well, and she seemed to me everything that a poet should be.

Her cordiality and her quick comprehension of things—it seemed to me that she understood at once whatever I mentioned to her—made me wish that I could stay there forever. Before I knew what I was doing, I was telling her all about Harriet Hurd and the sorrows and discouragements of my long courtship. She seemed to know all about that too, and I felt at once that I had never talked to any one so responsive. She asked me to bring Miss Hurd to see her some time, and some months afterward I did, with the greatest pleasure to both of us. That first visit to Mrs. Spofford began a friendship which has now lasted for more than thirty years.

Although my last interview with Miss Hurd at Marcy was a definite dismissal, I did not entirely give up hope. People never really give up hope when they desire anything greatly. As soon as I got work in Boston, I began hoping for a letter from her. I always went to the post-office down on Devonshire Street every Sunday; for there was no delivery on that day, and, if a letter did come from her, I could not take the chance of its lying over in the office until Monday. I always imagined there was a letter waiting there as I hurried down the street, and at the general delivery window I inquired impatiently, as if I knew it was there. The blank denial of the postal clerk never quite dashed me, and next Sunday I was in just as much of a hurry. At last a letter did come, to tell me she was returning some books I had given her; but the tone of it was friendly enough to make me resolve to try again.

After the *Wheelman* got fairly started the future looked brighter to me than it had ever looked before, and I began to go up to Andover, where Miss Hurd was teaching in Abbot Academy. I made the acquaintance of Miss Philena McKeen, the principal of the academy, and she became a warm friend of mine. She even urged, when at last Miss Hurd definitely decided to marry me, that we should be married in Andover, at the Academy. For, at last, Miss Hurd did decide.

Our engagement had been off and on now for about six years. She had made every reasonable concession to her father's strong feeling; she had waited, as he besought her to, had gone away from Galesburg, formed new friends, and neither seen me nor written to me for four years. Our feeling for each other had endured through so much, and survived so many vicissitudes, that she at last felt that it would be right to marry me, even against her father's wishes and though she knew that such a decision would cause him the bitterest disappointment.

After she once made up her mind it was the right thing to do, I knew that nothing could alter her decision, just as I knew that, if she had decided that it would be wrong, nothing on earth could have made her marry me. Before the spring term of 1883 was over, Miss Hurd wrote her father that she intended to marry me; that, if he wished her to be married at home, she would go home for the summer vacation and have her wedding in September. If he did not wish her to be married at home, she would not wait until fall, but would be married at the Academy, under Miss McKeen's directorship, as soon as the spring term was over. Professor Hurd wrote that he would rather she were married at home.

During the previous winter, in December, I came down with a severe attack of typhoid fever. I do not remember much about that illness, but Colonel Pope's twin sisters, both practising physicians in Boston, remember it perfectly. John Phillips, my brother John, and I were all living in one room somewhere in Boston. I had not been able to go to work for several days, and the boys reported me to Colonel Pope as ill. He called upon his sisters and told them he wished they would go to see me and do what could be done for me. Miss Pope says that she came to my room and found me well advanced in typhoid. She had me sent to a hospital and put in a private room, and she and her sister often came to see me and kept an eye on my progress. I recovered rapidly, remaining in the hospital only three weeks and two days. Colonel Pope paid all my hospital expenses, as well as my salary during the time I was ill.

It would probably have been better for me had I remained in the hospital longer, for I felt the effects of that illness all summer and my energy was below normal. Miss Hurd went back to Galesburg in June and I had a rather gloomy summer. My physical weakness showed itself in occasional fits of depression. Sometimes I got very far down indeed. At such times I used to feel sure that, although the date for the wedding was then set, it would never come off at all. I used to be overwhelmed by the certainty of losing everything. That summer I experienced the truth of the saying that a coward dies a thousand deaths.

When, at last, I went West to be married, Professor Hurd would allow me to call at the house only once before the actual ceremony. His students used to call him "the old Roman," and up to the moment his daughter left his house he did not disguise his hostility. From the first I had always had a great sympathy with Professor Hurd's attitude, and I understood his feeling better than he knew. I could appreciate his lack of confidence in me because I had never had any great confidence in myself. I realized perfectly well that he had every reason to expect a better marriage for his daughter. Every one in Galesburg expected a brilliant future for a girl so beautiful and gifted.

Harriet's attainments had been a great satisfaction to her father. In educating her he had demonstrated some of his pet theories. He had put her to work at Latin and Greek while she was still a child, and she had acquired an easy mastery of both languages at the age when most students are beginning them. He had sent her to Berthier-en-Haut for a year to assure her a fluency in French, and had spared no pains to develop a mind unusually gifted. Her beauty, too, and her beautiful speaking voice were matters of pride to him. It seemed to him that she would be entirely wasted on a visionary boy like me. All her friends felt the same way. Indeed, when Mrs. Williston, of Galesburg, first introduced me to Miss Hurd, she said, noticing my absorption when I sat next to Harriet at luncheon: "Don't cry for the moon, Sam." People in Galesburg tell me how often they used to notice Harriet Hurd out walking; she was very slender, had a free carriage, and walked straight, like an Indian girl.

Harriet and I were married at her father's house in Galesburg, September 4, 1883, seven years, lacking three days, from the date of our first boy-and-girl engagement. I had asked Harriet then whether, if I turned out to be a good man, she would marry me in seven years. I do not remember much about the ceremony, except that I broke in and said "yes" too soon, and then had to say it over again.

After the wedding we started East, going back to Boston by way of Quebec, where we spent some delightful days at a little French hotel. I was then making fifteen dollars a week. I had transportation over the railroads and sixty dollars in cash for

HARRIET HURD, WHO BECAME MR. MCCLURE'S WIFE AFTER AN
ENGAGEMENT OF SEVEN YEARS

THEODORE L. DE VINNE, FOUNDER OF THE
DE VINNE PRESS

ROSWELL SMITH, OWNER OF THE "CENTURY"

my wedding journey, and I was amazed that our week on the ᵣoad took it all. Indeed, I was so prudent about that sixty dollars that Mrs. McClure began to remember with apprehension a certain cautious professor at Knox College who had kept an itemized account of the expenses of his wedding trip.

We began to keep house in a little frame house in Wendell Street, Cambridge, where there were lots of ripe grapes in the back yard, I remember. Mrs. McClure had saved up three hundred dollars from her teaching, and with this she furnished the house. Our rent took just half of my salary, and we lived on the other half. Everything was going well.

About this time Colonel Pope decided to buy the magazine called *Outing* and combine it with the *Wheelman*, making Mr. W. B. Howland, the owner of *Outing*—afterward the publisher of the *Outlook* —business manager of the new magazine. Mr. Howland and I were to have equal authority in editorial and business matters.

I felt at once that this combination would not work out well for me, and that I could not edit a magazine where I shared the authority and responsibility with another man. Mrs. McClure and I went over to New York to apply for work on the *Century*. Mr. Roswell Smith, owner of the

Century, was then the foremost figure in the magazine world. I had made the acquaintance of the *Century* people when I bought the plates of the bicycling article which we republished in the first number of the *Wheelman*, and had since that time often met Mr. Chichester, the business manager of the *Century*. A connection with the *Century Magazine* was the uttermost limit of my ambition.

Mr. Smith gave my wife and me a cordial welcome, and talked to us as if he were an old friend. He encouraged us to tell him all about our affairs and promised to give us the best counsel he could. After we returned to Boston I received a letter from Mr. Smith strongly advising me to go into the De Vinne printing house and work my way up in that profession. The De Vinne Press was one of the best printing houses in the world, if not the best, and Mr. Smith said he could get me a position with Mr. De Vinne. He added that, if we needed money for the move to New York, I could draw on him to the extent of a thousand dollars.

So, three months after our marriage, Mrs. McClure and I left our first home in Cambridge and went to New York. We shipped our household goods, and we went down on a boat of the Fall River Line. It was late in December, and as we passed under Brooklyn Bridge on the morning of

our arrival the clouds were heavy in the sky. By
the time we landed the rain was falling in torrents
and the lights were burning in all the downtown
business houses. We had been directed to a miserable little boarding-house near Warren Street,
where we were wretchedly uncomfortable for a few
days. We soon found more comfortable quarters
in a lodging-house at 141 West Fifteenth Street,
where we had the parlor floor and the use of the
kitchen.

Mr. Smith had got me a place in the De Vinne
printing house at twenty-five dollars a week, and he
gave Mrs. McClure a position at fifteen dollars a
week on the Century Dictionary, which was then
in the course of preparation.

She went to her work every day as regularly
as I went to mine. Her work was to read
American authors and select sentences illus-
trating the usage of certain words for quotation in
the Dictionary. My work at De Vinne's was reading proof and measuring up what the compositors
had set. The hardest thing about it was that it
kept me on my feet all day, and I was still weak
from my illness of the winter before. I felt exactly
like a rubber ball that has been burned and lost all
its spring. The hours were long; I had to be at the
composing rooms every morning at seven o'clock,

and I had only half an hour for lunch. I used to sleep until the last possible moment in the morning, then throw on my clothes, put some rolls and raisins in my pocket, take the elevated at Fourteenth Street, and get down to Murray Street perhaps five minutes late, perhaps fifteen. We were timed as we went in and our tardiness was taken out of our pay. Mrs. McClure and I both worked until six o'clock at night, and then went home dead tired, and cooked our dinner and washed the dishes. Sunday was the only day when we ever saw each other by daylight.

From the first day I entered the De Vinne Press I knew that I did not want to become a printer. Everything about the work was distasteful to me. I remember one job I had was to prepare a catalogue for a loan exhibition of paintings in Brooklyn. I had to go around to the offices of a lot of rich men, bankers and manufacturers, who were lending pictures, to get my information. They sometimes kept me waiting for hours and then sent out word that I would have to come again when they were not so busy. I saw that it would take years to work up in the printing business. I was entered on the payroll as an expert printer—which I was not—and the wages of an expert printer were then eighteen dollars a week. To give me a chance, Mr. De

Vinne paid me seven dollars every Saturday night out of his own pocket. I could see no future, but, on the other hand, it seemed as if I must see the job through. In the half hour I had for my lunch, I used to go out to the City Hall Square, and look up in desperation at the sky and buildings, like a man in prison trying to find a way of escape.

I never spoke of my wretchedness to any one, but Mr. De Vinne was a kind man as well as a great expert, and he must have seen that I was not happy. When I had been with him for four months, he told me that I had better go up to the Century office and talk with Mr. Smith, intimating that they would be able to use me there. I had a talk with Mr. Smith and he took me on. Thus began my connection with the Century Company. Mr. William Ellsworth, the secretary of the Company, was away on his vacation, and I was given some of his work to do. The work that interested me most was writing announcements of the future numbers of the magazine. But, on the whole, I did not get on much better with my work in the Century office than I had at De Vinne's.

My wife had given up her work on the Dictionary some months before, and we had moved to East Orange, New Jersey, where in July my daughter Eleanor was born. I had arranged to take my two weeks' vacation then, so that I could be with Mrs. McClure and the baby. During those two weeks, for the first time since I came to New York, I began to recover myself, to get back my mind and to have ideas. During the six months of my imprisonment in office routine I had been like another man, a wholly different creature. As soon as I got away from office work, my powers of invention seemed to return to me. One evening in East Orange, I sat down and in a few hours invented the newspaper syndicate service which I afterward put through. I saw it, in all its ramifications, as completely as I ever did afterward, and I don't think I ever added anything to my first conception.

To be sure, the thing was in the air at that time: somebody had to invent it. The New York *Sun* had made a tentative experiment in that direction. Mr. Dana had arranged with a number of authors, among whom were Mr. Howells, Henry James, and Bret Harte, to sell him short stories which would appear in the Sunday *Sun*, and on the same day would be printed in Sunday papers in Chicago, St. Louis, New Orleans, etc. The Boston *Globe* had also sold a serial in this way.

In reading over the files of *St. Nicholas* for the Century Company to prepare for them a "Boys' Book of Sports," I had noticed a great many articles

and stories which I thought ought to be syndicated
in all the country newspapers throughout the land,
to supply good reading matter for the country boys
and girls. I had studied the files of the *Century*
carefully in preparing my announcements, and I
knew who was writing then and what they wrote.
I did not see why the Century Company should not
conduct a syndicate business, selling new stories by
their authors and old material from the files of *St.
Nicholas* to newspapers. During my vacation I
worked out a complete plan of such a syndicate
service, covering eighteen large pages, and when I
went back to work I submitted this prospectus to
Mr. Frank H. Scott, afterward president of the
company.

Mr. Scott gave my prospectus his friendly consideration and said he would lay it before Roswell
Smith. An hour or two after Mr. Smith called me
in, and said he didn't think I would ever get very
far working for the Century Company; that I did
not seem to be fitted to work to advantage in the
offices of a big concern; that he felt the best thing
for me to do would be to go out and try to found a
little business of my own. My salary would be
paid until the first of October, and I could have the
month of September to look around. If I found
nothing, Mr. Smith said, I could come back and

work with them that winter. This was certainly a generous proposition.

I was fortunate in my three employers. The only men I ever worked for—Colonel Pope, Mr. De Vinne, and Roswell Smith—were all remarkable men, each a master in his own line. Colonel Pope, while a boy in the army, had carried on his studies by the camp-fire, made a fortune in business within a few years after he came back from the war, and by the time he was thirty-nine had founded one of the great manufacturing concerns in America. Mr. De Vinne was then, and is to-day, one of the world's foremost experts, a wide scholar as well as a great printer. Mr. Smith was then the preëminent magazine publisher of America. Incidentally these men had made fortunes, but they had also made great names. They were all men who could inspire a young man, who valued ideas above the price they brought in the market, and who were not ashamed to have ideals.

The more I thought about the syndicate idea, the more I believed in it. It became an obsession with me. Again I was a man of one idea, as I had been when I was determined to get an education, as I had been when I was determined to get my wife. Every one with whom I discussed the idea manifested a great indifference.

If I were going to launch a new venture, I had, of course, to have a New York address. In October we moved in from East Orange and took a flat at 114 East Fifty-third Street. When we paid the month's rent in advance, twenty-three dollars, it left us almost penniless. We had four rooms, two with sun, facing on the south, and two facing on a very clean court behind the Steinway piano manufactory. We had two sleeping-rooms, a kitchen, and one other room which was my office as well as our sitting-room and dining-room. I got a large old-fashioned desk and put it between the two windows in that room. I went downtown and bought white paper in bulk, having it cut up into the sizes wanted for letter paper. It was months before I had any printed stationery. I had always liked the purple ink which the Century Company then used for business correspondence—this was before the general use of typewriting machines—so I laid in a supply of purple ink. Then I sat down and began to write letter to authors and editors, explaining to them my syndicate scheme.

From the authors I got immediate and enthusiastic replies. They would be delighted to be syndicated, would be delighted to write for me. But the editors were much more cool in their replies. It was then I learned that the selling end of any business is the difficult end.

My plan, briefly, was this: I could get a short story from any of the best story-writers then for $150. I figured that I ought to be able to sell that story to 100 newspapers throughout the country, at $5 each. News was syndicated in this way, and I did not see why fiction should not be.

I launched the syndicate November 16, 1884. The first thing I syndicated was a two-part story by H. H. Boyesen. I had agreed to pay Boyesen $250 for it, and although some newspapers in large cities paid as high as $20 for the right to print it, my returns on the story aggregated $50 less than the story cost me. This was a serious situation, as I was not only $50 behind, but I had no money to live on.

I went down to the Century office and borrowed $5 from a young man I had worked with there— it must be remembered that I knew almost no one in New York—and with this $5 I went to Philadelphia. There I sold two stories, the one by Boyesen and another by "J. S. of Dale," for $45 to Philadelphia papers. I borrowed some money from a relative there, and went on to Washington, where I also sold my stories, then home. As soon as I got back to New York, I went to Boston. There Mr.

Howland, of *Outing*, got me a pass to Albany. Because of some limitation to my pass I had to stay overnight in North Adams, and I got the editor of the little paper there to agree to take my syndicate service of one short story a week for $1.50 a week. At Albany I sold the service for $5 a week.

When I got back to New York I found letters from several important newspapers, such as the St. Paul *Pioneer Press* and the San Francisco *Argonaut*—which I had written to but had not heard from before—agreeing to take the service at $8 a week. Then I realized that I was started. I paid Boyesen part of what I owed him, and lived on the rest, paying him a little more, as I could. Week after week and month after month I fell short in this way, and got deeper and deeper into debt. I got along by paying my authors $10 or $20 on account. I paid out a little less than I collected, and my actual working capital was the money I owed authors. I made no secret of this, and the men who wrote for me were usually willing to wait for their money, as they realized that my syndicate was a new source of revenue which might eventually become very profitable to them. And it did.

CHAPTER VI

HARD SLEDDING—GETTING THE SYNDICATE ON
ITS FEET—MY FIRST AUTHORS—HENRY
HARLAND AND THE "YELLOW BOOK"—I WRITE
A SERIES OF ARTICLES ON COOKERY—GETTING
SYNDICATE IDEAS—MY FIRST CALL UPON
STEVENSON—THE OFFER FOR "ST. IVES"—
WE PLAN THE SOUTH SEA CRUISE—HENRY
JAMES AND STEVENSON—STEVENSON'S WILL-
INGNESS TO BE EDITED—STEVENSON'S WIFE

This was my situation during those first months
that I was starting the syndicate. I was twenty-
seven years old, with a wife and baby; I had no
business friends or connections in New York;
and I was launching a new business that had never
been tried before. I was utterly without resources.
I had not $25 in the bank, and I had no relatives who
could help me. At the end of the first week of the
syndicate I was $50 behind. I passionately be-
lieved in the idea, but there were times when *I
knew that it could not succeed because too much
depended upon it.* It wasn't as if I had had money
enough to live on for six months while I gave the

thing a trial. We had not even a day's credit at the grocery shop. We were cooking on a one-burner oil-stove, an old one, badly worn, and I did most of the washing in order to save my wife.

I was sure enough of the idea, but I was not sure that I was the man who could carry it out. There seemed no chance for anything new. Surely, I used to tell myself, if the thing were worth doing, somebody would have done it before. I used to go out and walk about the city, anguishing over the thing. New York looked full; the world looked full. What chance was there for a little new business with no capital behind it, with only one young man behind it? And I had less confidence in that young man than I had in any other, because I knew him better than I knew any other man. I looked about over a city of six-story buildings—great stretches of the upper West Side were unoccupied, and Harlem was a country district—a city lit by gas, where all the cars were drawn by horses except the elevated trains, which were pulled by little steam-engines; and it seemed as if everything had been done, as if there were no further possibilities of expansion.

Every young man has to face and overcome that delusion of the completeness of the world. It is like a wall too high to climb over, a hedge too dense to wriggle through. The Columbia College buildings were then on Forty-ninth Street, very near our flat, and I used to get so low in my mind that I would go over there and try to get a job in the Library. I remember, at one time I agreed to select and file newspaper clippings for the librarian for $3.50 a week. These fits of desperation came on when I had no money to get out of town to see editors, no chance to extend the business or to talk over my ideas with newspaper men. There is nothing like the enthusiasm and appreciation of another mind to help a new idea to develop.

I remember, one Saturday afternoon Mrs. McClure and I started for a walk in Central Park. I was wheeling the baby in the carriage, and we were talking about what we were going to do to get provisions to last over Sunday. I had no money at all, and, as I have said, we had no credit. As we left the apartment-house I was met by the postman with a registered letter. It contained an unexpected ten-dollar bill from a paper in New Orleans. We felt as if the future were provided for.

I never kept books; a few notes jotted down from time to time kept me informed as to my accounts. I had never had a bank account before, and I was always having to pay out an extra dollar and a half for fees on over-drafts. I paid my authors as I

could. Some writers were very agreeable about
waiting, and others were not so long-suffering.
Once, when I was out of town selling my stuff to
editors, Edgar Fawcett's valet came to our flat,
and sat there all day for three days in succession
to collect for a story of Fawcett's. Mrs. McClure
told him she had no money, but he came back just
the same.

When I made up my accounts on the first of
April, five months after the syndicate was started,
the various newspapers I served owed me $1000,
and I owed $1500 to authors. Just at that critical
time a two-part story came in from Harriet Prescott
Spofford, with a note saying that this story was a
present—that she had meant it for a New Year's
present, but she hoped it wouldn't be too late.
That story was like a buoy thrown to an exhausted
swimmer, that holds him up until he can get his
breath. I sold it for $275. On the first of June
my accounts showed a balance of $161 in my
favor.

And yet, all this time we were very happy. I
was rich in ideas and in hope, and my wife believed
in my ideas and in me. Mrs. McClure attended
to all the business when I was off on my trips to see
newspaper editors. She wrote a great many of my
business letters, prepared copy for the printers,

and translated French and German short stories, which I sold in my regular syndicate service. Postage was one of the heavy drains upon our purse, and when we had to decide between postage stamps and steak for dinner, she always declared for the postage.

At one stage of the game we took a "mealer," a fine young man whose sister had been a fellow teacher of Mrs. McClure's at Abbot Academy. He helped us cook on a new gas-burner, and accommodated himself to our circumstances with great zest. Once, when I was starting off on a trip to encourage the editors, I wore one high shoe and one low one, because the mates of both were unfit to be seen. On that same trip I had the misfortune to lose $45 in cash—simply lost the stuff. I was always careless about money, and in Cincinnati I had $45 which I had that day got from the Indianapolis *News*, in my trousers pocket, along with some stamps. I pulled out the money and stamps to mail a letter, and never saw the money again. I had to borrow money to get home on from the editor of the Cincinnati *Commercial Gazette*. When I reached home and told Mrs. McClure about it, we decided to have a good dinner and forget it. We had a saying, in our flat, that if you didn't *mind* a thing, it never really hurt you. We were never crushed or poor in spirit. We never let our poverty make us mean. That is the greatest hurt that poverty can inflict upon people. Once the syndicate got fairly started, after it had lived a few months indeed, I was sure that I could make it go. After that I was seldom discouraged. I was doing the work I loved and developing my own idea, and so always felt cheerful. So did my wife.

I had no vacations except Sunday, and then Mrs. McClure and I usually took the baby and went off on a boat somewhere, or walked in the Park. Our real pleasure, however, was the new business itself. We had it there in the flat with us; we ate in the office; the syndicate was a member of the household. Mr. Grady, editor of the Atlanta *Constitution*, came to the flat to see me on business about this time, and he wrote an article on the contiguousness of my business and domestic operations, saying that the dinner and the baby and the ink-bottles were inextricably confused.

Between us, Mrs. McClure and I did every kind of office drudgery, all the things that in an ordinary business there are half a dozen people to do. We did the office-boy's work and the clerk's work and the stenographer's work. Our office hours were from eight in the morning to ten o'clock at night. When things were all at sixes and sevens, and the business seemed to be fairly tumbling about my ears, I have sat down after dinner at night, and written by hand as many as forty letters to editors, outlining glowing plans for the future operations of the syndicate. The risks were always immediate and great. Even after I was selling to newspapers enough to feel that I could count on a profit of $50 a week, a paper taking $25 service was likely at any time to discontinue its patronage, taking half of my net profits.

When I was serving, say, forty papers, forty copies of the story for any given week had to be sent out, and the copies for the Pacific Coast papers had to be mailed ten days before the date of their publication. Making these duplicates was always a harassing question. If I had had them set by a job printer and galley proofs run off, the cost of composition would have more than eaten up any possible profits. So it was my custom to supply the service free to one newspaper that would set from the author's copy and supply me with the requisite number of galley proofs to be sent to the other newspapers, where the story was set up for each paper from these proofs. Often the paper that supplied these proofs would be late; sometimes, after I had spent an anxious day or two waiting for them, they would come just in time for me to rush them off on the first mail. Sometimes they would be too late altogether for the more distant papers, and I would lose heavily for that week, and perhaps lose the patronage of a paper that had been disappointed. So we lived in turmoil.

Among my first authors were George Parsons Lathrop, Frank R. Stockton, Julian Hawthorne, Harriet Prescott Spofford, H. C. Bunner, Louise Chandler Moulton, and Henry Harland, who became famous about that time as the author of "As It Was Written," a novel which he published under the name of Sidney Luska. Harland was the son of a New York lawyer. He afterward went to England and became editor of the *Yellow Book*, considered a very bold publication in those days, a rather daring book to have on one's table. Every one remembers his success with "The Cardinal's Snuff Box."

Edmund Clarence Stedman introduced me to Harland when his first novel, "As It Was Written," was being talked about everywhere. Harland was working in a downtown office then, and he did his writing at night. He often used to write until four o'clock in the morning. He was a young man of twenty-four or twenty-five then, with a manner at once ingratiating and sincere, an inveterate smoker of choice cigarettes. I bought some of his short stories for the syndicate, and serialized one novel, "The Yoke of the Thorah." All his early stories were about Jewish life.

Harland had been married but a short while, and was living in his father's house on East Fifty-fourth Street, one of a row of houses overlooking the East River. Mrs. McClure and I got to know him and his wife very well. We were all young people starting out in life, and most of the men with whom my business brought me in contact were older men, already established, like Mr. Stedman, Mr. Howells, and Mr. Stockton. As for the older editors, they all believed that there would never be any new magazines in the world—that *Harper's* and the *Century* and the *Atlantic* could consume all the stories that would ever be written in America, and that if I went on buying stories for my syndicate there would not be enough to go around. Harland and I looked at some of these things differently, and we found a good deal in common. One summer, when he and his wife went away, Mrs. McClure and I lived in their apartments on the upper floors of the Harland house.

After Harland went to England he changed greatly, and he quite outgrew his early stories. Once, when I went to see him at his place in Kensington, I threatened to republish all of his Sidney

Luska stories under his own name. "If you do, Sam," he said, "I'll publish a statement that Sam McClure is the author of every one of them!" Harland and his *Yellow Book* set were so far advanced at that time that they considered George Meredith very old-fashioned indeed. When I objected to the ethics of a story published in the *Yellow Book*, Harland rolled on the floor with laughter. "The same old Sammy!" he chuckled. "The same old Sammy!" But, in spite of their advanced ideas, the *Yellow Book* did not rejuvenate English fiction. The new movement had begun in quite another quarter, and was identified rather with the name of Robert Louis Stevenson.

The last time I ever saw Harland was in San Remo, Italy. He was as delightful a companion as ever. I noticed that he had shaved off his moustache, and I asked him why he had done it. He smiled drolly and said: "Sam, the darned thing was getting white!"

The summer that I was living in Harland's apartments, I was writing a series of cookery articles for the syndicate, signing myself "Patience Winthrop," and hoping that under this pseudonym I would be taken for a New England housewife. The newspapers were just beginning to publish cookery articles at that time; it was a new thing;

and mine were very successful. It came about in this way. When we were married, Mrs. McClure, having always been a student and teacher, did not know how to cook. After the syndicate got a little start and we began to have time to take such things into account, I went to the kitchen of the Astor House and learned how the best cooking in New York was done. I learned how to do a few things as well as they could be done, and learned a few basic principles—for instance, that meats should be cooked slowly, by a moderate heat, that eggs cooked for eight minutes in water below boiling heat (at 170° F.) are much better than eggs cooked for two minutes in boiling water.

After my syndicate had been going for a year, I felt that I could afford to take a downtown office. I rented a room in the Morse Building, on the corner of Nassau and Beekman streets, opposite the Tribune Building, and hired a stenographer. Among the people who wrote for me at this time were Octave Thanet, Elizabeth Stuart Phelps, Mrs. Burton Harrison, Sarah Orne Jewett, Brander Matthews, Joel Chandler Harris, Charles Egbert Craddock, and Margaret Deland.

After the syndicate had been running for two years, John S. Phillips came home from Germany. When we left the *Wheelman* in Boston, Mr. Philips

S. S. MC CLURE IN 1885

JOHN S. PHILLIPS

had gone to Harvard for two years, and after taking his degree there had gone to study at Leipsic. He remained there a year, and then came to New York, where he joined me in the syndicate business coming in at a salary, and becoming my partner in the business seven years afterward. When Mr. Phillips joined me, I was under the impression that I was about $1800 ahead, but, on making a careful examination of my affairs, he discovered that I was only $600 ahead. I drew no specified salary from the business; I owned the syndicate, and I simply took out money as I needed it. A very bad method; for, while I thought I was taking about $3000 a year for my family expenses, I was probably taking out $4000 or $5000. Expenses were heavy during those years, as my four children were born between 1884 and 1890.

Mr. Phillips very soon took over the entire office management of the business, for which he was much better fitted than I. He had an orderly and organizing mind—which I had not—and he had had a much wider education. I usually lost interest in a scheme as soon as it was started, and had no power of developing a plan and carrying it out to its least detail, as Mr. Phillips had. His extraordinary competence in the office left me free to move about the country, seeing editors and authors and keeping in touch with both ends of the market. I found out what people were writing and what people were reading, and in which of the happenings in the world people took the keenest interest. Often I was able to suggest to writers a subject profitable to them and to me. I sometimes spent as many as seventeen successive nights in sleeping-cars, when I was traveling for the syndicate. I never got ideas sitting still. I never saw so many possibilities for my business or had so many editorial ideas as when I was hurrying about from city to city, talking with editors and newspaper men. The restlessness which had mastered me as a boy always had the upper hand of me, and it was my good fortune that I could make it serve my ends. Whatever work I have done has been incidental to this foremost necessity to keep moving.

Of course, as soon as my syndicate began to pay, other syndicates were started. The most powerful of these was started by Allan Thorndyke Rice, editor of the *North American Review*. My friends and many of the editors I served thought such a competitor would be too much for me. I remember that at this time Miss Sarah Orne Jewett, who wrote for the syndicate and took a friendly interest in my business, wrote me to ask whether I could not form some combination with Mr. Rice to avoid being wiped out. Mr. Rice's syndicate was very strong for a time, but eventually it died out without seriously cutting into my business. At one time the St. Jacob's Oil people organized a syndicate service, furnishing matter to the newspapers for $75 a week and guaranteeing to place with each paper that took the service advertising of their oil enough to cover the cost of the service, thus giving it to the paper for nothing. This sounded formidable, but I was sure it would not succeed, for I knew there was small likelihood of the St. Jacob's Oil people finding an editor who could buy such material as would be of any value to the newspapers. And, indeed, their syndicate had but a short life.

The Bacheller Syndicate, organized by Mr. Irving Bacheller, author of "Eben Holden," proved to be my strongest competitor. In 1887 I heard that Mr. Irving Bacheller was going abroad to get material from English writers, and I thought I had better go also. Before I sailed, Charles de Kay, brother-in-law of Richard Watson Gilder, told me about a very remarkable story of adventure, "Kidnapped," that had been published in England. I read the book, was greatly delighted with it, and as soon as I got to London, in February, 1887, I wrote to the author at Bournemouth, where I understood he was staying for his health. To this letter I got no reply. But late in the summer of that year, a young man came into my office in the Tribune Building, in New York, asked to see me, and introduced himself as Lloyd Osbourne. He said he was the stepson of Robert Louis Stevenson, and that Mr. Stevenson had received a letter from me which he had never been able to answer because he had mislaid it and did not remember the address; but that Stevenson was in New York, at the Hotel St. Stephen on Eleventh Street, and would be glad to see me.

Mrs. McClure and I called upon Stevenson, accordingly, and were taken to his room, where he received us in bed, very much in the attitude of the St. Gaudens medallion, for which he was then posing. We had a pleasant call, but there was nothing very unusual about it. Stevenson, though he was in bed, did not seem ill; he looked frail but not sick. The thing about his appearance that most struck me was the unusual width of his brow, and the fact that his eyes were very far apart. He wore his hair long. Stevenson was already a famous man; the publication of "Dr. Jekyll and Mr. Hyde" had made him so.

I did not see him again before he went to the Adirondacks. In October I went up to Saranac to see him, commissioned by Mr. Pulitzer of the *World* to offer him $10,000 a year for a short essay every week, to be published in the *World*. He had already such a "news value" as to be worth that to a paper.

Brander Matthews had told me about three long adventure stories that Stevenson had published in *Henderson's Weekly*, an English paper of about the character of the New York *Ledger* in this country. These stories were "Treasure Island," "Kidnapped," and "The Black Arrow." He had received only $500 apiece for them. They had not appeared over his own name, but were signed with his pseudonym, "Captain North." I believe some of his literary friends in England were very much opposed to his publishing adventure stories, such as "Kidnapped," under his own name, as they thought it might compromise his future.

"Kidnapped" and "Treasure Island" had already been republished in book form, but "The Black Arrow" had never been resurrected, and lay unknown to the world in the back files of *Henderson's Weekly*. When I went up to Saranac for Mr. Pulitzer, I told Stevenson that I would publish "The Black Arrow" serially in my newspaper syndicate, and pay him a good price for it. Mrs. Stevenson was not at home then, and Stevenson said he could not decide the matter without consulting her, as she had never liked the story, and he thought she might be unwilling to have it republished under his own name. She never was much in favor of the project, but gave her consent.

Stevenson had no copy of the story, but he sent to England and got the files of *Henderson's Weekly* which contained the story, and sent them to me. I read the story, and told him that I would take it if he would let me omit the first five chapters. He readily consented to this. Like all writers of the first rank, he was perfectly amiable about changes and condensations, and was not handicapped by the superstition that his copy was divine revelation and that his words were sacrosanct. I never knew a really great writer who cherished his phrases or was afraid of losing a few of them. First-rate men always have plenty more.

Stevenson's news value was such that it was a great thing for the syndicate to be able to offer the newspapers a serial of adventure by Robert Louis Stevenson. But we had no copyright law then, and if I published the story under its original title, "The Black Arrow," any American paper might cut in, get a file of *Henderson's Weekly*, and come out ahead of me. In the hope of keeping possible pirates in the dark, I advertised and published the story under the title "The Outlaws of Tunstall Forest." I had it illustrated with line drawings by Will H. Low, an old friend of Stevenson's since their Barbison days. That was the first illustrated story we ran in the syndicate, and it brought in more money than any other serial novel we ever syndicated.

While it was running in the syndicate under a new title, Stevenson arranged for the book publication of "The Black Arrow" with Charles Scribner's Sons. His friend William Archer went over the proofs for him in October. It was in April of that year, at Saranac, that he wrote the dedication of the book, inscribing it to Mrs. Stevenson, the "Critic on the Hearth."

"No one but myself," this dedication begains, "knows what I suffered, nor what my books have gained, by your unsleeping watchfulness and admirable pertinacity. And now here is a volume that goes into the world and lacks your *imprimatur;* a strange thing in our joint lives; and the reason of it stranger still! I have watched with interest, with pain, and at length with amusement, your unavailing attempts to peruse *The Black Arrow;* and I think I should lack humor indeed, if I let the occasion slip and did not place your name in the fly-leaf of the only book of mine that you have never read—and never will read."

While the preparations for this were going on, I went up to Saranac several times to see Stevenson. He was living in the Baker cottage, a rented furnished house near an ice-pond with trees around it. I remember once I took up a pair of skates for him and a pair for myself, and we skated. He was then going over Lloyd Osbourne's story, "The Wrong Box." Osbourne had written the story throughout, and Stevenson went over it and touched it up. I read it, and thought it a good story for a young man to have written; but I told Stevenson that I doubted the wisdom of his putting his name to it as joint author. This annoyed him, and he afterward wrote me that he couldn't take advice about such matters. He told me, during that visit, that he had two new novels in mind, one of them a sequel to "Kidnapped." The other was "St. Ives." I told him that I would take either story and pay him $8000 for it. He blushed and looked confused and said that his price was £800 ($4000), and that he must consult his wife and Will Low before he made any agreement. He went on to say that he didn't think any novel of his was worth as much as $8000, and that he wouldn't be tempted to take as much money as that for a novel, if it were not for a plan he had in mind. He was always better at sea, he said, than anywhere else, and he wanted to fit up a yacht and take a long cruise and make his home at sea for a while.

When I left Saranac that time, Stevenson had agreed to let me have the serial rights of a novel for $8000. About two weeks later he wrote to his friend Charles Baxter:

"I am offered £1600 [$8000] for the American serial rights on my next story! As you say, times are changed since the Lothian Road. Well, the Lothian Road was grand fun, too; I could take an afternoon of it with great delight. But I'm awfu' grand noo, and long may it, last!'"

His exultation, however, was short-lived. When he made this agreement with me, he was already under contract with Charles Scribner's Sons to let them handle all his work in this country. Two days after the above letter to Baxter, he wrote to Mr. Charles Scribner:

"Heaven help me, I am under a curse just now. I have played fast and loose with what I said to you, and that, I beg you to believe, in the purest innocence of mind. I told you that you should have the power over all my work in this country; and about a fortnight ago, when McClure was here, I calmly signed a bargain for the serial publication of a story. You will scarce believe that I did this in mere oblivion; but I did; and all I can say is that I will do so no more, and ask you to forgive me."

Some weeks later Stevenson wrote to Henley:

"I have had the most deplorable business annoyances too; have been threatened with having to refund money; got over that; and find myself in the worse scrape of being a kind of unintentional swindler."

The novel that finally fulfilled this contract between Stevenson and me was "St. Ives." At the time when I made it, I knew nothing of his agreement with Scribner's. He was the last man to inform one about his business affairs, even when he was informed as to them himself, which was not often. He says, in a letter to Mr. Burlingame, editor of *Scribner's Magazine*, written shortly after he made this contract with me:

"I have no memory. You have seen how I omitted to reserve the American rights in "Jekyll"; last winter I wrote and demanded as an increase, a less sum than had already been agreed upon for a story that I gave to *Cassell's*. For once that my forgetfulness has, by a cursed fortune, seemed to gain, instead of lose, me money, it is painful that I should produce so poor an impression on the mind of Mr. Scribner."

"STEVENSON RECEIVED US IN BED, IN THE ATTITUDE OF THE ST. GAUDENS MEDALLION"

MRS. ROBERT LOUIS STEVENSON

ROBERT LOUIS STEVENSON

The evening of the day on which I offered Stevenson an increase in his serial rates was the first time I ever heard him talk of his desire to take a long ocean cruise. He told me again that he didn't think his novels were worth what I had offered him, and that the consideration which most influenced him to accept such a price was his wish to take a yacht and live for a while at sea. I thought at once of "An Inland Voyage" and "Travels With a Donkey," and told him that if he would write a series of articles describing his travels, I would syndicate them for enough money to pay the expenses of his trip. I think the South Seas must have been mentioned that evening, for I remember that after I returned to New York I sent him a number of books about the South Seas, including a South Pacific directory. The next time I went to Saranac, we actually planned out the South Pacific cruise, talking about it until late into the night.

That was a night not easily forgotten. Stevenson's imagination was thoroughly aroused. He walked up and down the floor, or stood leaning against the mantel, inventing one project after another. We planned that when he came back he was to make a lecture tour and talk on the South Seas; that he was to take a phonograph along and make records of the sounds of the sea and wind, the songs and speech of the natives, and that these records were to embellish his lectures. We planned the yacht and the provisioning of the yacht, and all possible adventures. We planned a good deal more than a man could ever accomplish, but it was all real that night, and out of that talk came the South Sea cruise. That was just before I went to London to syndicate "The Outlaws of Tunstall Forest" in England, and I never saw Stevenson again. When I returned to New York from London, he was in San Francisco, fitting out the yacht *Casco* before his departure to the South Pacific, from which he never returned.

His "South Sea Letters" ran for about a year in the syndicate. They were, on the whole, a disappointment to newspaper editors, for they revealed a side of Stevenson with which the public was as yet not much acquainted. There were two men in Stevenson—the romantic adventurer of the sixteenth century, and the Scotch Covenanter of the nineteenth century. Contrary to our expectation, it was the moralist and not the romancer which his observations in the South Seas awoke in him, and the public found the moralist less interesting than the romancer. And yet, in all his essays, the moralist was uppermost.

Stevenson was the sort of man who commanded

every kind of affection; admiration for his gifts, delight in his personal charm, and respect for his uncompromising principles. Underneath his velvet coat, his gaiety and picturesqueness, he was flint. It was probably this unusual combination of qualities in him that made one eager to serve him in every possible way. I remember saying to Mr. Phillips once: "John, I want the syndicate business to be run exactly as if it were being conducted for the benefit of Robert Louis Stevenson." And that was the way I felt about him.

Before I sailed for London, Stevenson gave me letters to a number of his friends there—Baxter, W. E. Henley, Sidney Colvin, R. A. M. Stevenson, and others. I found most of Stevenson's set very much annoyed by the attention he had received in America. There was a not of detraction in their talk which surprised and, at first, puzzled me. Henley was particularly emphatic. He had a double grievance: that a nation whom he despised as a rude and uncultivated people should presume to give Stevenson a higher place than he held in England, and the personal jealousy which he later voiced in his own writings. He believed that his own influence upon Stevenson's work was not sufficiently recognized. Some of Stevenson's London friends agreed that he was a much overrated man, and that his cousin, R. A. M. Stevenson, was the real genius of the family.

There was one most marked exception to this dissenting chorus, and that exception was Henry James, to whom Stevenson had given me a letter. I had somehow always imagined Mr. James as a rather cold and unsympathetic man, but I now found how greatly I had been mistaken. His tone about Stevenson warmed my heart. His warm human friendship was a delight after what I had been hearing. There was nothing at all critical in his attitude. He was Stevenson's friend, admirer, and well-wisher. His interest in Stevenson's health, his work, his plans for the future, was wholly affectionate, wholly disinterested. His loyal, generous feeling I have never forgotten. He questioned me minutely about everything pertaining to Stevenson. His interest was keen, sympathetic, personal.

During that visit to London I learned to appreciate one of Stevenson's great sources of discouragement. Some of his friends there, those in whose critical powers he had most faith, were always condemning his new book, whatever it was. They could stand for what was already printed, but when he sent them the manuscript of a new work, they usually declared that that was fatal, that would be the end, and entreated him, for the sake of his reputation, not to publish it. One benefit of his life in the South Seas was that it placed him farther from these inhibiting influences, and left him freer to work out what was in him as best he could in the short life allotted to him.

Although some of Stevenson's friend were jealous of him in a small way, most of them were jealous for him in a very high way. Serious men took him more seriously than they took other writers of fiction. Critics like Mr. Colvin felt that he had a very precious gift, something to be preserved for the highest uses. He was not judged with the same leniency as other writers of his time. These criticisms of his friends were often the highest expressions of their solicitude and regard; they were often very helpful to Stevenson, but sometimes disheartening. He was so sensitive to the opinions of others that an office-boy could influence him, for the moment. And yet, in the long run, he could not be influenced at all. But this suscepti-bility, the fact that he could be so easily discouraged by criticism, sometimes brought him great mental suffering.

When Stevenson began to send in his "Letters from the South Seas," he told me to use my own judgment about editing them, and to cut wherever I thought it would be advantageous. After the series was well started in the syndicate, he wrote and asked me why I was not cutting the stuff down more. I have mentioned this willingness to be edited before, and I have said that all of the really first-rate writers I have known have been similarly open-minded. I must mention it again, because, somehow, young writers often have the idea that they are lowering their flag if they consent to any changes in their manuscript—that there is a mystic power in a certain order of words. My experience has been—and I think all other editors have had the same experience—that only writers of inferior talent and meager equipment feel in that way. To a man of large creative powers, the idea is the thing; the decoration of phrase is a very secondary matter. He has no feeling that, because he has set a thing down one way once, it must stand so forever. He can say the same thing in fifty different ways. If his story is loose and runs thin, he is glad to tighten it. If it is congested, and he has tried to bring out too many points, he will cut. He can afford to spare a few ideas; he has plenty. He has no feeling that he can not cut out this sentence because he will never be able to say that particular thing so well again; he knows he'll say it better. I mention Stevenson particularly, because he is acknowledged to have been an artist in words and to have achieved a more finished style than most men, and had a very particular regard for style in its high sense. But he would have been very much ashamed of a style that condensation could hurt. He often lamented that Balzac did not have somebody to edit and condense his novels for him.

In "The Dynamiters" Mrs. Stevenson actually collaborated with her husband, and she was a very strong influence in all of his work. Her criticism and suggestions had at all times great weight with him. All his more important work was done after his marriage.

The more I saw of the Stevensons, the more I became convinced that Mrs. Stevenson was the unique woman in the world to be Stevenson's wife. Every one knows the story of their first meeting: how, when Mrs. Osbourne was traveling in France with her daughter, Stevenson one afternoon, passing in the street, happened to look into the dining-room window of the little hotel at Grez just as Mrs. Osbourne was rising from the table; how he looked into her face for a moment, and said, when he went on up the street, that there was the only woman in the world he would ever marry.

There had been a Spanish ancestor somewhere back in Mrs. Stevenson's family, and in every other generation the strain asserted itself. She herself is a very marked Spanish type. When Stevenson met her, her exotic beauty was at its height, and with this beauty she had a wealth of experience, a reach of imagination, a sense of humor, which he had never found in any other woman. Mrs. Stevenson had many of the fine qualities that we usually attribute to men rather than to women: a fair-mindedness, a large judgment, a robust, inconsequential philosophy of life, without which she could not have borne, much less shared with a relish equal to his own, his wandering, unsettled life, his vagaries, his gipsy passion for freedom. She had a really creative imagination, which she expressed in living. She always lived with great intensity, had come more into contact with the real world than Stevenson had done at the time when they met, had tried more kinds of life, known more kinds of people. When he married her, he married a woman rich in knowledge of life and the world. Mrs. Stevenson's autobiography would be one of the most interesting books in the world.

She had the kind of pluck that Stevenson particularly admired. He was best when he was at sea, and, although Mrs. Stevenson was a poor sailor and often suffered greatly from seasickness, she accompanied him on all his wanderings in the

South Seas and on rougher waters, with the greatest spirit.

A woman who was rigid in small matters of domestic economy, who insisted upon a planned and ordered life, would have worried Stevenson terribly. In his youthful tramps he liked to start out with no luggage, buying a collar here and a shirt there, as he needed them. In managing his affairs, he had, as he often said, no money-sense. I remember hearing him tell how he and Mrs. Stevenson once went to Paris for a pleasure trip. They had a £100 ($500) check and some odd money, and they meant to have a thoroughly good time and stay as long as their money held out. After a few days they found their funds running short; they couldn't imagine what they had done with it all, but there seemed to be very little money left, so they decided they had better get home while it lasted. When they got home, they found the £100 check among their papers. They hadn't cashed it at all, and didn't even know they hadn't.

In spite of his carelessness about money, and the fact that he put about $20,000 into his house in Samoa, Stevenson did so much work, and the demand for it has been so constant, that he left a large estate. A sick man of letters never married into a family so well fitted to help him make the most of his powers. Mrs. Stevenson and both of her children were gifted; the whole family could write. When Stevenson was ill, one of them could always lend a hand and help him out. Without such an amanuensis as Mrs. Strong, Mrs. Stevenson's daughter, he could not have got through anything like the amount of work he turned off. Whenever he had a new idea for a story, it met, at his own fireside, with the immediate recognition, appreciation, and enthusiasm so necessary to an artist, and which he so seldom finds among his own blood or in his own family.

After Stevenson disappeared in the South Seas, many of us had a new feeling about that part of the world. I remember that on my next trip to California I looked at the Pacific with new eyes; there was a glamour of romance over it. I always intended to go to Samoa to visit him; it was one of those splendid adventures that one might have had and did not.

One afternoon in August, 1899, I went with Sidney Colvin and Mrs. Sitwell (now Mrs. Colvin) to Paddington station to meet Mrs. Stevenson, when, after Stevenson's death, she at last returned to Europe after her world-wide wanderings, after nine years of exile. There were only the three of us there to meet her. She had come from Samoa by way of Australia, and was to land at Plymouth from a P. & O. liner. When she alighted from the boat train, I felt Stevenson's death as if it had happened only the day before, and I have no doubt that she did. As she came up the platform in black, with so much that was strange and wonderful behind her, his companion through so many years, through uncharted seas and distant lands, I could only say to myself, "Hector's Andromache!"

I got into an embarrassing predicament through syndicating Stevenson's "Outlaws of Tunstall Forest" in England in 1888. Mr. Tilleston, a hard-headed old Yorkshireman, had the largest syndicate business in England, and I had an agreement with him that I was to syndicate his serial novels in America, and he, in return, was to syndicate mine in England. Up to this time no American novel had been syndicated in England, and as I had never had occasion to fulfill my end of the agreement, I had forgotten all about it. When I came to handle Stevenson's adventure story, I went to London and began to place the story myself. Mr. Tilleston promptly called me to account, and we had an interview at the National Liberal Club in which he not only demanded the English returns for the Stevenson serial, but all the profits I had made on syndicating Tilleston material in America. I was so remorseful and so eager to make amends for my breach of faith that I consented to this, though it was a rather hard bargain, and paid Tilleston a sum which wiped out a large share of whatever I had ahead.

I then immediately borrowed £100 of Tilleston, and went with Mrs. McClure on a pleasure trip to Italy. This was my first experience of Italy, and those were wonderful days. When we got to Florence, we found Timothy Cole, the engraver, there, at leisure and disposed to be our companion in our visits to the galleries. He went with us again and again to the Pitti, the Uffizi, and the Belle Arti, talking enchantingly about the pictures. His companionship was a great piece of good fortune for me, as well as a great pleasure. I had never before had time or opportunity to look at pictures, and that ten days in Florence opened a new world to me. From Florence Mrs. McClure and I went to Rome. That is always a great experience for any one who has cared about his classics in college. When I got to the Forum, I felt as if Caesar had been there yesterday.

The next year, 1889, I was serializing Rider Haggard's novel "Cleopatra" in the syndicate. Some years before this, when "King Solomon's Mines" was first published in England, Brander

Matthews had told me to look up this new man, Haggard. Brander Matthews has always been a man of catholic taste, such as seldom goes with a critical ability of such a high order as his, and he has always kept abreast with and been in sympathy with new literary movements, however foreign they may be to his personal taste. He has always brought an unprejudiced attention to any new literary manifestation. And Haggard was the first to sound the new note in English fiction which was to make itself heard above everything else for years to come. (I do not count Stevenson here. He was a man apart; he belonged to no school.) Before Haggard came out with a new tune, we had only the old English novel, become mechanical and in its decline—the stories of Wilkie Collins, James Payn, Mrs. Braddon, Clark W. Russell. In contrast to these, "King Solomon's Mines" was a fresh breath from a new quarter of the world.

During my visit to London in 1889 I went up into Scotland, to visit Andrew Lang at St. Andrew's. Andrew Lang was then literary adviser for Longmans, and while we were talking together he remarked that Longmans were about to bring out a new novel, "Micah Clarke," by a man named Conan Doyle, who had already published a shilling-shocker called "A Study in Scarlet." On the train, going down from Scotland, I bought the shilling-shocker at a news-stand, and as soon as I had read it decided to go after Doyle's stories for the syndicate. It used to be said of me in those days that all my geese were swans, because I went after things so hard.

I bought the first twelve Sherlock Holmes stories from Mr. Watt, Conan Doyle's agent, and paid £12 ($60) apiece for them. I had but one test for a story, and that was a wholly personal one—simply how much the story interested me. I always felt that I judged a story with my solar plexus rather than my brain; my only measure of it was the pull it exerted upon something inside of me. Of course, sometimes one is influenced by one's own mood; if one is feeling more than usually vigorous, he is apt to transfer some of his own high spirits to the story he is reading. To avoid being influenced thus, I always made a rule of reading a story three times within seven days, before I published it, to see whether my interest kept up. I have often been carried past my station on the elevated, going home at night, reading a story that I had read before within the same week.

When I began to syndicate the Sherlock Holmes stories, they were not at all popular with editors. The usual syndicate story ran about five thousand

SIR A. CONAN DOYLE

RUDYARD KIPLING

words, and these ran up to eight and nine thousand. We got a good many complaints from editors about their length, and it was not until nearly all of the first twelve of the Sherlock Holmes stories had been published, that the editors of the papers I served began to comment favorably upon the series and that the public began to take a keen interest.

Shortly after this I was in London, and one day when I was going somewhere in a cab with Wolcott Balestier, he told me that Doyle had just completed a new historical novel, "The White Company." I bought the American serial rights of the novel for $375; but when I sent the proofs of it around to the newspaper editors, they simply would have none of it. This, it must be remembered, was after the publication of the twelve Sherlock Holmes stories. I went to Mr. Laffan, of the New York *Sun*, and told him I had a novel of Doyle's I couldn't sell. Mr. Laffan took it off my hands and serialized it in the *Sun*.

This was one of the most interesting of all my trips to London. I was lunching one day with Sidney Colvin at the British Museum, where he was in residence as Curator of Prints and Engravings. Colvin told me about a new writer who seemed to have red blood in him, and who had done a good deal of work out in India that was beginning to be talked about in London. His name, Colvin said, was Rudyard Kipling. The name was so unusual that I had to write it down to remember it.

Shortly after this I paid my first visit to George Meredith. I went to Box Hill to see him about getting the right to syndicate several of his novelettes, such as "The Tale of Chloë," which had never been published in book form and were unknown in America. During the course of our conversation I said:

"Mr. Meredith, Mr. Colvin thinks very highly of a new writer named Rudyard Kipling. He believes he is the coming man. Do you know anything about him?"

"The coming man," said Meredith emphatically "is James Matthew Barrie."

Neither Meredith nor Colvin was far wrong.

CHAPTER VII

HELP FROM AN UNEXPECTED SOURCE—ON THE
EDGE OF BANKRUPTCY—GEORGE MEREDITH—
THE NEW WRITER

It was about eight years after I had founded my newspaper syndicate business that I first began seriously to consider founding a magazine. The originators of the cheap magazine in the English-speaking world were, I should say, the late Sir George Newnes, editor of the *Strand* and *Country Life,* and William T. Stead, whose great career was ended by the *Titanic* disaster. The success of Newnes' magazines and Stead's *Review of Reviews,* and the success of the *Ladies' Home Journal* at ten cents in this country, made me think that a cheap popular magazine would be possible in the United States.

The development of photo-engraving made such a publication then more possible. The impregnability of the older magazines, such as the *Century* and *Harper's,* was largely due to the costliness of wood-engraving. Only an established publication with a large working capital could afford illustrations made by that process. The *Century Magazine* used, when I was working for it, to spend something like five thousand dollars a month on its engraving alone. Not only was the new process vastly cheaper in itself, but it enabled a publisher to make pictures directly from photographs, which were cheap, instead of from drawings, which were expensive.

Early in 1892 Mr. Phillips and I began to plan actively to launch a new fifteen-cent monthly. The name of the new publication bothered me not a little. I thought of calling it the *New Magazine*, the *Galaxy*, or *Elysium*. Finally Edmund Gosse said: "Why not call it *McClure's Magazine?*" That was the name we decided upon.

Our entire capital at that time was $7300, and of this Mr. Phillips had put in $4500. So, after eight years of the hardest kind of work in the syndicate business, I was only $2800 ahead. I had begun to see that there was not much further growth to be hoped for in the syndicate. We had important rivals by this time, and they cut down our profits. The only practical expansion was in the direction of a magazine. In spite of our small capital, I thought I could make a magazine go. In place of capital, we had a great fund of material to draw from.

The magazine at first was to be made entirely of reprints of the most successful stories and articles that had been used in the syndicate. We had then about two thousand short stories in the safe to draw from, and I meant to reprint only the best of them. It was clear to me that for the first year or two the staff of the new magazine would have to live on the profits of the syndicate. If we paid the salaries out of the returns from the syndicate, and cut the cost of the material we printed by using reprint matter almost altogether, I thought the new publication might be made to pay for its own paper and printing. Consequently we had to arrange as big a year as possible for the syndicate.

Early in 1892 I went abroad to get the best material for the syndicate that I could find in England, and Mr. Phillips did the same in this country. We made contracts with writers many times in excess of our entire capital. On my return from London, I crossed the continent to the Pacific, and visited all the important newspapers between the Atlantic and Pacific, placing the new syndicate material.

On my way East, I stopped at Davenport, Iowa, where my old college friend and classmate, Albert Brady, was the publisher of the Davenport *Daily Times*. I had watched his remarkable work there for some years, and I believed that he was the one man I knew who could become advertising manager of the new magazine. I engaged him at a salary of $5000 for five years, his first year's salary being more than two-thirds of our entire capital at the time.

Just before the first number of *McClure's* came out, I was in the West, pushing the syndicate for all it was worth. I was sitting in the office of my friend Mr. Nixon, editor of the Chicago *Inter-Ocean,* one day, when a telegram was handed me. It was from Mr. Phillips, and asked me to collect from *Inter-Ocean* for last month's syndicate service. I tore the telegram into small bits and dropped them into the waste-paper basket. Later I remarked casually that if it were convenient I should like a check for the last month's service. Mr. Nixon smiled.

"Money? Oh, no! We can't give you any money. Look out there!"

He pointed to the window, and I looked out. Down below I saw a crowd in the street, masses of people seething from curb to curb before a building. The building was a bank. That was the first I saw of the panic of 1893. And the first number of the new magazine was not yet off the presses. Mr. Phillips, in New York, had seen what was coming, and had wired me to get hold of any money I could.

But there was none to get. The ordinary sources of money were frozen.

The panic was like no other panic of recent years. It was largely a result of the Sherman Act for the compulsory coinage of a fixed amount of silver, which had been passed some years before and had resulted in a general hoarding of gold as against silver money. If you had a great deal of money in the banks, you could draw out only a small portion of it. Wherever money was, there it stuck; the flood of currency was actually congealed. We could not collect from the newspapers that owed us; indeed, we were glad enough to wait for our money, if only we could keep their patronage.

As soon as the newspapers felt the pinch of the panic, they began to cut down expenses, and our syndicate service was one of the first things they could dispense with. One paper after another wrote us to say that they would have to discontinue taking syndicate matter. Every discontinuance meant a net loss to us of from twenty to seventy dollars a week. Before we had got over the shock caused by the loss of one of our best customers, another letter would come saying, "No more syndicate matter until times are better." There was certainly never a more inopportune time to launch a new business.

One of the articles in the first number of the magazine was a popular science article on evolution —"Where Man Got His Ears," by Professor Henry Drummond. Professor Drummond was then in Boston, delivering the Lowell Lectures. I usually forgot my financial anxieties, even when we were in the direst straits, in the pleasure I always got out of the editorial end of my work—hunting new ideas and new writers, and, as it were, introducing them to each other. So, before the first number of the magazine was out, I went to Boston to see Professor Drummond, to arrange with him for further popular science articles for the magazine. I had first met him in the early days of the syndicate, when he had delivered at Columbia a lecture on his explorations in tropical Africa, incidental to his study of the slave trade there. Later we became well acquainted, and I visited him in Glasgow.

When I saw Professor Drummond in Boston, I did not say anything about my own financial anxieties, but we spoke of the panic. He told me that his Lowell Lectures on "The Descent of Man" had been very successful, and that the hall had been so crowded that he had been forced to give each lecture twice. He had therefore received a good deal more than the usual fee. He asked me whether I happened to need any money. I thought he meant for immediate personal expenses, and, thanking him, told him I did not. He went on to say that if $3000 would be of any assistance to me in my business, he could just as well let me have his check from the Lowell Institute, which was for that amount. When I told him that I did indeed need money, he made his check over to me, taking $2000 worth of stock in the new magazine and advancing me the other thousand as a loan. It seemed curious that, when all ordinary springs of money were dry, money should have come from a source that a financier would hardly have thought of.

That $3000 from Professor Drummond enabled me to get out the next two numbers of *McClure's Magazine*. But the money stringency did not relax. I had to get more funds to get out the fourth and fifth numbers.

I was lucky enough to buy for two hundred and fifty dollars a new serial novel by an unknown writer that went well in the syndicate and helped us along. It was "A Gentleman of France," by Stanley Weyman, and was one of the most successful novels we ever handled, bringing us in about $2000.

We began to issue *McClure's Magazine* with fixed charges in excess of all possible returns from the syndicate business. The first number came out at the end of May, 1893. We printed 20,000 copies, and of these 12,000 were returned to us. The 8000 that were sold brought us in about $600, while the paper and printing had cost thousands. The newspaper notices of the new publication, however, were exceedingly cordial and friendly. I believed that we could eventually make the thing go, if only we could keep it alive for a few months. But how to keep it alive was the question. Small businesses were being wiped out every day. There were weeks when I used to look in the evening paper every night to see whether we were posted in the list of bankrupts. I used to imagine how six issues of the magazine would look if they were stood up in a row, but I was very doubtful as to whether we could ever publish that many.

I ran up to Boston again, and went to my old friend and employer, Colonel Pope. He gave me a check for $1000, to be taken out in advertising. On his advice, I went to Mr. Hollingsworth and persuaded him to extend me a month's credit on paper. When I returned toNew York I got a month's credit from the printer. Houses that had never extended credit before were forced to do so when money was so scarce.

Another difficulty arose in the shape of unexpected competition. Our June number was our first issue. The next month, the *Cosmopolitan*, then edited by Mr. John Brisben Walker, cut to 12½ cents, 2½ cents under *McClure's*. I had thought that it would be a year or two before there was another cheap magazine in the field. Nevertheless, in one way and another, always on the edge of failure, we got through the hard fall and winter of '93–94'. Colonel Pope came to the rescue again at one critical time, and advanced me $5000 on advertising.

In the spring of 1894, when the magazine had been running nearly a year, I went to London to buy material for the syndicate, without money. We were then owing to English authors about $3500, which we were absolutely unable to pay. Of course, our credit there was suffering seriously, and that was a grave thing for us, as much of our best syndicate fiction came from England. While I was in London that spring, H. J. W. Dam came to me, and told me that he must have the hundred dollars I owed him for an article. He said he was about to be put out of his flat, and before he got through talking he actually cried. I cried too, but I had no money to give him.

When I returned to New York in the early summer of '94, we were running the magazine at a loss of $1000 a month. By cutting the text of the magazine from 96 to 88 pages for several months, and reducing the size of the illustrations, I reduced this loss somewhat; but financially we were not succeeding. As the summer went on, things got worse and worse. Our indebtedness to English authors increased from $3500 to $5000, and I could see no prospect of reducing it. I had gradually exhausted all my sources of capital. I had got as much money as possible from Colonel Pope, as much credit as possible from the paper manufacturer, Mr. Hollingsworth, and from the printer. There was no one left to whom I could turn for further money or credit. Mr. Phillips had already put in as much money as he could raise by inducing his father to mortgage his home in Galesburg. I felt, day after day, as if I were trying to walk into a granite wall.

Mrs. McClure and I were living at Bayshore, Long Island, that summer. One cloudy afternoon, when I was on the train going home from the city, I looked up from the manuscript I was reading, and noticed that the weather had lifted and that the sun was shining. Instantly I felt an unaccountable rise of spirits. The next morning, before hurrying away to catch my train, I told my wife that there was no possible chance for our success unless God helped us. Every human source of help was exhausted,

MRS. S. S. MC CLURE

S. S. MCCLURE'S MOTHER

and without help we could not go on. I asked her to pray God to help us. She said that I must pray also; but I told her that she could pray better than I could.

Conan Doyle was at this time lecturing in America. On that day he was staying at the Aldine Club. I had been so weighed down by business cares that I had not seen him since his arrival in the United States, and I had a feeling of having neglected him. Prompted by this feeling, I went that morning directly from the station to the Aldine Club. In apologizing to him for my seeming indifference to his presence in America, I told him that I had been upset by business anxieties, remarking incidentally that I had to finance the magazine as well as edit it. Conan Doyle then said that he would like to put some money into the business himself, if I needed it; that he believed in the magazine and in me. I lunched with him at the club, and after lunch he walked over to the office with me, and wrote out his check for $5000, exactly the sum we were owing to English authors. When that check was written, it put new life into the office staff. Every one in the office felt a new vigor and a new hope.

It was in that critical spring of 1893, also, that I first met Miss Ida M. Tarbell, who afterward played such an important part in the history of

McClure's Magazine. One day I noticed on Mr. Phillips' desk a proof of an article signed "Ida M. Tarbell." The article was on "The paving of the Streets of Paris by M. Alphand." I picked it up and read it. When I had finished it, I said to Mr. Phillips: "This girl can write. I want to get her to do some work for the magazine." The article possessed exactly the qualities I wanted for *McClure's.*

So, early in the spring of 1893, the year that *McClure's Magazine* was started, when I was in London buying material, I went over to Paris to see Miss Tarbell. I called upon her at her little apartment on the river, taking with me some newly discovered information about the Brontës upon which I wished to get her judgment. I went to see her, intending to stay twenty minutes, and I stayed three hours. The following year Miss Tarbell wrote several articles for *McClure's*—one on Professor Janssen and his Observatory on the top of Mount Blanc, and one on the Bertillon system for the identification of criminals, which virtually started the interest in that system in the United States.

As I watched Miss Tarbell's work I saw how much she had benefited by her study of the methods of French historians, then so much in advance of our own. I was at once convinced, too, of the soundness of her judgment. So, desperate as were the financial straits of the magazine, my admiration for her work led me, when I was in London the next spring, to offer her a salaried position on *McClure's Magazine*. She needed a hundred and fifty dollars to settle up her affairs there and pay her passage to America, and this I somehow managed to advance her.

Shortly before Miss Tarbell began her work on the magazine, a letter came into the office from a man in Omaha, suggesting that we publish a series of portraits of Napoleon for our "Human Documents" series. That seemed to me a good idea, so I began to look about for portraits of Napoleon. I heard from W. E. Curtis that Mr. Gardiner Hubbard, of Washington, the father-in-law of Professor Alexander Graham Bell, had a remarkable collection of Napoleon pictures; so, returning from a trip on syndicate business, I stopped at Washington. I reached Mr. Hubbard's residence, Twin Oaks, at nine or ten o'clock in the morning. He had been collecting his prints and engravings for eleven years, and in half an hour after he began to show me his collection all the desks and tables and chairs of his library and the adjoining room were covered with pictures of Napoleon, a complete pictorial history of the Emperor's career. Mr. Hubbard was most willing to let me reproduce his collection in the magazine, but he agreed with me that there should be an accompanying text, a brief history of Napoleon.

My first effort to procure this text failed completely. I commissioned a young Englishman to do it, and when his article came in I took it down to Mr. Hubbard. We went over it together, and decided that it would never do. Then I told him about Miss Tarbell—of her work in Paris, and how well she had covered the period preceding Napoleon in her "Life of Madame Roland." Mr. Hubbard was favorably impressed by what I told him, and thought it would be well to give her a trial of this piece of work. I went back to New York, and telegraphed Miss Tarbell, who was visiting her parents at Titusville, asking her whether she would go to Washington and write a Life of Napoleon. My telegram touched her sense of humor by its very improbability, and she replied that she would.

The year 1894 was a Napoleon year. In November the *Century Magazine* began its "Life of Napoleon," by Professor Sloan, which they had been preparing for years, and the same month we began our "Life of Napoleon," got up, as it were, overnight. Within a few months our circulation rose from 40,000 to 80,000.

The inception of Miss Tarbell's "Life of Lincoln"

was almost as casual. The idea occurred to me of having a series of articles on Lincoln, written by many different men who had known him, and of having Miss Tarbell edit these articles, bring them into scale with one another, and herself write in the portions of Lincoln's life that these articles did not cover. I soon found, however, that this plan would not succeed, and that, if a piece of work is to be well done, one person must do it. In the light of her success with the Napoleon, it was clear that Miss Tarbell was the one to write our "Life of Lincoln" with as much fresh material as she could get. The portraits of Lincoln that were sent into the office were invaluable as clues to the sources of new material. The portraits of Lincoln came from all sorts of obscure sources; people sent them in from all over the country, and in our correspondence about them we formed an intimate personal connection with people in all parts of the country, often with people who had never read magazines before. We published many portraits of Lincoln that had never been published before. One of these, taken in his early youth, caused a great sensation.

This "Life of Lincoln" told on our circulation as nothing ever had before. In August, 1895, our circulation was 120,000; in November, 1895, it had risen to 175,000; in December, 1895, it was 250,000.

In two years and a half from the founding of *McClure's Magazine* we had reached a circulation far in excess of the *Century, Harper's,* or *Scribner's,* and soon to be greater than all three. But we had gained in standing and esteem as well as in circulation, and the years '95–'96 actually put *McClure's Magazine* on the map. A new sense of hope came to all of us. The uncertainty and dread that we had lived under for so long passed away.

In our access of confidence, we overstepped ourselves. For our January number, 1896, we overprinted so far that we had about 60,000 returned copies on our hands. I also launched a *McClure Quarterly,* the first number containing our collection of Napoleon pictures, and the second containing the first four instalments of Miss Tarbell's "Early Life of Lincoln." The *Quarterly* never got beyond the first two numbers, for on those we lost many thousands of dollars. We were losing money, moreover, on account of our enormous increase in circulation. Most of our advertising contracts were made on a basis of 40,000 to 80,000 circulation. We had taken on an unprecedented body of advertising at a low rate, and now we were printing 250,000 magazines a month, with the enormously increased cost of manufacture which such a large printing entailed, and we were getting no more for our advertising than if we were printing only 80,000 copies a month.

By the first of January, 1896, we decided to have a printing plant of our own. Mr. Hollingsworth agreed to give us fifteen months' credit for paper. He also influenced the manufacturers of printing-presses in our favor, and we got a printing plant on credit. We began the year 1896, then, $287,000 in debt. I was thirty-nine years old, had been out of college fourteen years, and I had never been out of debt.

Throughout the year 1895, with our low-rate advertising contracts and increasing circulation, the magazine was losing $4000 a month. In 1896 it was clearing over $5000 a month. Its prosperity and standing had been established.

We had accomplished a greater success than it would have seemed reasonable to expect. During the first summer of the magazine's existence, in the panic year of '93, I was staying with Professor Henry Drummond at Northfield, where he was visiting Moody's school. We took long walks together; and one day, when we were off in the country, sitting on the grass, I told Drummond that I did not see how I could possibly put through the task I had undertaken—that I did not feel strong enough to do it, and that I always seemed to be undertaking more than I could do. I have never forgotten his reply. He said: "Unless a man undertakes to do more than he possibly can do, he will never do all that he can do."

The editorial history of *McClure's Magazine*, in the early chapters, was certainly more cheering than its financial history. From the first number, the press and the public received it warmly. My old newspaper friends throughout the country were exceedingly generous in their notices and reviews of the publication. It was recognized from the first as a new note in journalism, individual and distinctive. Among the contributors to our first number were H. H. Boyesen, Gilbert Parker, Sarah Orne Jewett, Professor Henry Drummond, Joel Chandler Harris, Gertrude Hall, and Mrs. Robert Louis Stevenson. One of the distinctive features begun in the first number was a series of "Real Conversations," carefully prepared interviews with noted men about their life and work. The first of these was an interview with William Dean Howells, by H. H. Boyesen. Later came interviews with Eugene Field, Frank R. Stockton, Jules Verne, Alphonse Daudet, Professor Alexander Graham Bell, and many others.

The "Human Document" series, begun in the first number of *McClure's*, was another feature, so successful that we would have kept it up forever if the supply of great men had held out. This series was christened by Alphonse Daudet. When Mr. Jaccaci, art editor of the magazine, was in Paris, he explained to Daudet our intention of publishing in each number a series of photographs of some noted man, from his youth up.

"*Veritables documents humaines!*" exclaimed Daudet; and we adopted that title for the series.

We made, I think, a more serious effort in the direction of popular science articles than had been made by any magazine before us. *McClure's* was the first popular journal to announce Marconi's discovery of wireless telegraphy, and when that article appeared it was generally regarded with utter incredulity. I remember, a professor of Clark University wrote on that occasion and urged us to avoid announcing such absurdities and thereby making the magazine ridiculous. As late as 1908, when we published the first authentic article on the Wright Brothers' flying-machine, then unknown to the world, people merely thought we had been imposed upon. It is sometimes as useless, from a news point of view, to announce a thing too early as to announce it after every other magazine has had it.

The "Human Documents" series led to many

interesting personal contacts. In 1895 I went to Germany to get a series of the best portraits of Bismarck, and I spent two days with his son, Count Bismarck, at his great farming estate, Schaffhausen, not far from Magdeburg.

Count Herbert Bismarck, at the time I visited him, was a man in middle life. He was, I should say, typical of great men's sons—a man of some force, but overshadowed by his father. He took me to a little building on the estate which was used as a museum in which were kept all the presents sent to his father from all over the world. I saw a great many curious and interesting things, but the thing I best remember was a cabinet photograph of the present Emperor, taken when he was a boy, and sent by him to Bismarck while his grandfather was still on the throne and his father was an apparently sound man with the prospect of a long reign before him. On this photograph was written, in young William's hand, "*Cave adsum.*"

Count Herbert called my attention to this photograph, but neither by word nor manner did he comment upon it. When I asked him what his father had said when he received this picture, Count Herbert replied imperturbably: "My father said nothing that it would have been unbecoming to say of his future Emperor."

The first distinguished series of short stories we published in *McClure's Magazine* were "The Heart of the Princess Osra" stories, by Anthony Hope. When I was in London on one occasion, Robert Barr, who often gave me valuable advice, told me that I would make a mistake if I left England without seeing Anthony Hope Hawkins, a new man who was doing remarkably interesting work. The day before I sailed for New York, Mr. Hawkins presented himself at my London office with a black valise full of his manuscripts and published works. I was in a hurry, and I told him I wouldn't bother about the manuscripts then, but that I would gladly take his books along and read them on the steamer.

I read "The Prisoner of Zenda" on my way across the Atlantic, and as soon as I got to New York I cabled Hawkins to send me all the manuscripts he had. The next time I was in London, Hawkins sent me the eight "Princess Osra" stories in a bunch. Mrs. McClure and I were staying with Mr. and Mrs. Robert Barr then. I took the manuscripts to his house, and after dinner in the evening Mr. and Mrs. Barr and my wife and I sat down in the library, and each of us took a "Princess Osra" story to read. Very soon some one exclaimed, and then some one else exclaimed. Each of us declared that the story that had fallen to his lot must be the best of the collection.   We each of us read the whole set that night, and we agreed that they were all real stories.

The next summer, 1894, Kipling's verse and "Jungle Book" stories began to take an important place in the magazine.   Kipling had several years before returned from India by way of the United States, writing, on his way, a series of letters ("American Notes") for the Allahabad *Pioneer*, the paper in India on which he had worked as reporter. The great body of Kipling's wonderful early work had then already been done.   All the stories that go to make up "Plain Tales from the Hills," "Soldiers Three," "Mine Own People," "The Phantom Rickshaw," and "The story of the Gadsbys" had already been published in Indian newspapers and afterward printed in paper-covered books.   These were the products of that prodigal period of early youth when the only thing that holds a genius back is that there are not hours enough in the day for him to write down the stories that are boiling in him.   And yet, he was as obscure to the world in general as any other young man who might have come out of the East with a bag of manuscripts.   Nobody had any idea that he was to be one of the great figures in English literature.

On his way to England, Kipling stopped a few

days in New York, and submitted his entire early
output, the books I have mentioned and others, to
Harper Brothers. They turned down the whole
mass of it, not accepting a single story. I think he
tried no other American publishing house, but took
his stories and went on to England. When I first
met him, soon after his arrival in London, he was
writing "The Light that Failed," for which Lip-
pincotts paid him $800, and which I afterward
syndicated.

He was still writing with the free pen of the
unknown man; he had achieved, as yet, only a
succès d'estime. Indeed, so far as the market was
concerned, Kipling went slowly. For a long while
his prices remained very moderate. He returned to
England, and began to be talked about there in
1887; but, as late as 1893, I was offered one of the
"Jungle Book" stories for $125. Five years later
I paid $25,000 for the serial rights of "Kim." We
also serialized "Captains Courageous" in *McClure's
Magazine.*

There was even a feeling of resentment on the
part of some of the older writers, who wrote about
the usual kind of thing, that these young men hailing
from foreign ports and out-of-the-way places of the
world should be attracting so much attention. Their
vogue was merely because their material was exotic,

some critics said. There was a rhyme going about among self-satisfied people:

> When the Rudyards cease from Kipling,
> And the Haggards Ride no more.

I have never seen the perverse side of Mr. Kipling that the American press at one time exploited. I doubt whether any one but the reporter has ever seen that side. He has always resented newspaper interviews. He has always refused to take himself as a public man, and has therefore felt that he ought to be exempt from interviews. His brusqueness with reporters is really an expression of his modesty. I have always found him cordial and tolerant of other people's interests. I remember he once told me, in London, that when I went to see him in Vermont I had "talked *McClure's Magazine* to him for eight solid hours." And he bore it! He used to say to me: "McClure, your business is dealing in brain futures."

Once, when I went to see him at Lakewood, he asked me whether I had read "David Harum." I replied: "No. He's dead."

Kipling laughed and said: "That's right, McClure. The mark of genius is to eliminate the unnecessary."

I first went to see George Meredith in 1890, and

arranged to publish several of his novelettes in my syndicate. Shortly before that I had read all of Meredith's published novels in rapid succession. I had always heard of Meredith as a man very difficult to read; his novels were spoken of as quite unattainable to the man of average intelligence. I had imagined that to read one of his novels would be something like reading a very obscure work on philosophy and psychology in one. Stevenson was the first man I ever heard speak of them as if they were interesting as well as profound. Once, when I was on the road, I bought a cheap copy of "The Egoist," and read it with the most intense interest. Then I read "Richard Feverel," after which I bought the set of eleven volumes in a box, and went straight through them. I was living then on Sixty-first Street. I read them on the elevated—before breakfast—while I was eating my lunch at the Astor House. I went through them in about six weeks, and had never read any novels with more interest or delight. I resolved to see Meredith the next time I was in London.

Sidney Colvin gave me a letter to Meredith, and Meredith wrote me, asking me to come out to Box Hill and spend the night. I went down on New Year's day of 1890, got off at the station in the afternoon, and went up the lane toward Meredith's house, approaching the gate with a good deal of shyness. Meredith himself met me. He walked slowly, even then, because of his nervous malady. I remember particularly his clear, ringing voice. His daughter was staying with him, and at dinner she sat at the end of the table opposite him, and a good deal of the conversation was directed to her. She did not attempt to answer his sallies in kind, but occasionally exclaimed indulgently, "Oh, papa!" His conversation was very like the dialogue in his novels; one had the feeling, when he talked, that there were swords flashing in the air.

After dinner we went up a steep hillside to his châlet. There were two settles there on either side of a roaring fire, and we sat down and talked about his novels until two o'clock in the morning, going from book to book and from character to character. During this talk I asked him how, in the light of his own experience, he would define genius. As nearly as I can remember, he said:

"It is an extraordinary activity of mind in which all conscious and subconscious knowledge mass themselves without any effort of the will, and become effective. It manifests itself in three ways— in producing, in organizing, and in rapidity of thought."

Before we went to bed that night, Meredith read

PROFESSOR HENRY DRUMMOND

GEORGE MEREDITH

me some chapters of an unfinished novel which he had begun seventeen years before and laid aside.

A year or so later I went to see Meredith again, this time taking Mrs. McClure. We were shown into a reception-room which I had not seen before. Over the mantel hung a painting of a beautiful girl. I said at once to my wife, "That was Lucy Feverel." I do not know whether it was Meredith's wife or not. At that time Meredith was very much interested in a translation of Homer that he was making, and he recited long passages of the Iliad in Greek.

When I got back to London after my first visit to Meredith, I told Mr. Frank Doubleday, who was then with Charles Scribner's, about this unfinished novel, and told him I believed that Meredith was on the verge of a wide popularity in the United States. Doubleday went down to see Meredith, and later Scribner's commissioned Meredith to finish the novel for *Scribner's Magazine*, where it was serialized under the title "The Amazing Marriage." Scribner's also took over the publication of all Meredith's novels from Roberts Brothers, a Boston house that published Stevenson and Meredith when they were unknown in this country, as well as introducing many of the great French and Russian writers into this country.

When I founded *McClure's Magazine* without money, my real capital was my wide acquaintance with writers and with what they could produce. My qualifications for being an editor were that I was open-minded, naturally enthusiastic, and not afraid to experiment with a new man. The men I tried did not always make good; but when they failed it never hurt anybody, and when they succeeded it helped every one concerned. A new writer gets to the people quickly enough, if he can once get by the editor. I was always easy to get by. If I believed in a man, I could give him a large audience at once; I could give him that gaze of the public which is the breath of life to a writer. Just as Niagara Falls was soundless until a human ear heard it, a writer does not exist until he is read. Kipling did not exist for New York when he first came through on his way back from the East, although he had a great part of his best work with him and actually in print. When we began to publish that first wonderful Kipling stuff, it seemed as if there would never be an end to it. I remember going from Lovell's to my own office with my arms full of Kipling galleys.

I could give a new writer such an instrument of publicity as had probably never been built up before. Through my newspaper syndicate I could place him at once before a million families, the representative

ANTHONY HOPE HAWKINS

BOOTH TARKINGTON

people who read the leading dailies in all parts of the country. The test of a writer's market value is, how many people will read him? I could give a new writer that test at once. The magazine and syndicate combined were the machinery I offered to get the young men in whom I believed to the people. The experience of those years taught me to say to young writers who brought me manuscripts and told me what this or that critic had said of his work: "The only critic worth listening to is the publisher— the critic who backs his judgment with his money."

That was an extraordinary group of young writers with whom I had to deal, but I did not realize it then. I needed good writers in my business, and it did not occur to me that they would not go on forever. I supposed that every ten years or so a new crop of such men came along.

Is the supply continuous? People often ask me whether I think there are unknown Kiplings and Stevensons working in obscurity. That I can not answer. But of one thing I am sure, and that is, if they are here, they do not at all resemble Kipling or Stevenson. Emerson said: "When a great man dies, the world looks for his successor. He has no successor." No more has a great writer. A group of great writers, like those of whom I have spoken, seem to exhaust the air for a time. It is usually fifteen or twenty years before a new man comes along who has really anything to say; and there must be a new race of critics and editors, too, who will permit him to say something new. The men of small talent unconsciously imitate the last great successes, and editors are looking for something like Stevenson or like Kipling, that will meet with the same success.

Kipling once said to me: "It takes the young man to find the young man." And that is true. The new talent is usually discovered by the editor who faces the future without predilections and without a gallery of past successes. No man's judgment retains that openness for very many years. His successes become his limitations. He is influenced by the development of his own tastes, by the memory of past pleasures, by the great personalities who have made the most interesting chapters of his life. His eyes are fixed on things behind him and soon become blind to the new man.

CHAPTER VIII

The "Muck - raking" Movement — The Standard Oil Articles—The Municipal Government Articles—Miss Stone's Story—
The Montessori Method—Mr. Turner's
Chicago Articles—The Commission Form
of Government

A T the time of the World's Fair there was established the Armour Institute of Technology
under the charge of Dr. Gonsalus, the great preacher.
I sent Arthur Warren to Chicago to write for *Mc-
Clure's* an article on the Armour Institute and on
Mr. Armour. That gave me the idea of having
articles written on the greatest American business
achievements, and it was suggested in the office that
the business achievements and methods of the Standard Oil—more especially, the great care that had
built up their methods of economical handling and
distribution—would afford a very interesting article.
Then, as we got into the subject, we saw three or
four articles, and planned, I think, to begin about
February, 1897. About that time the talk about
the trusts had become general—it was an important

subject. The feeling of the common people had a sort of menace in it; they took a threatening attitude toward the Trusts, and without much knowledge. So, in our office discussions, we decided that the way to handle the Trust question was, not by taking the matter up abstractly, but to take one Trust, and to give its history, its effects, and its tendencies.

Now the most important Trust was the first Trust and the great Trust, which, from its enormous wealth and through the ability of its founders and owners, might be called the Mother of Trusts. Many other trusts were subsidiary to this Trust. It was either the mother of the other Trusts, or the model, or the inspirer of them all. Moreover, it was the creature largely of one man, one figure, one personality—John D. Rockefeller. So that the history of this Trust would lend itself almost to the simplicity of biographical treatment. Miss Tarbell had lived for years in the heart of the oil region of Pennsylvania, and had seen the marvelous development of the Standard Oil Trust at first hand, so Miss Tarbell undertook to prepare some articles on the history of the Standard Oil, dealing especially with Mr. Rockefeller as the central figure. Mr. Rockefeller was well worth being the central figure —there is no question that he is the Napoleon among business men. Without him there would have been no Standard Oil. In the commercial, industrial and financial development of this country he probably played a greater part than any other single man. When the Standard Oil people learned of our project, Mr. H. H. Rogers sent us word through his friend, Mark Twain, that the Standard Oil people would gladly help us in securing material, and would lend us every facility for the production of this history. Miss Tarbell discussed each particular case with Mr. H. H. Rogers and showed him in advance of publication one article in which he was especially interested.

After these articles began to appear in *McClure's Magazine*, people were continually asking me where Miss Tarbell got her material; there seemed to be a general impression that she must have some mysterious source of information. It is true that she got material from many persons then living; but, in the main, her sources of information were open to any student who had the industry and patience to study them—the records of Congressional investigations, of State investigations, the testimony of Mr. Rockefeller, Mr. Archbold, and other officers of the company given in the suits that had been brought against the Standard Oil Company in different States. She also had access to many collections of material made by men who had fought the Standard Oil, and by lawyers who had conducted cases against the Trust. Through Mr. Rogers she had access to the information possessed by the Standard Oil people themselves. Her study of the wealth of accessible material lasted for five years, and enabled her to produce a history of unimpeachable accuracy.

The first important result of the publication of the Standard Oil series, was the change in regard to railroad rebates. It was realized that the railroad rebate was the great weapon of the Standard Oil.

Miss Tarbell had spent nearly three years on this work before the first chapter of it was printed. She had read and digested almost a library of material, and had traveled and seen a great number of people. When she wrote this "History of the Standard Oil" she was probably the greatest living expert on that subject.

Simultaneously with the beginning of the Standard Oil series, began the articles by Steffens on municipal misgovernment. Mr. Steffens had done some articles successfully for the magazine and had been asked to join the staff as desk editor. It seemed to me that he would be better qualified for the position if he became familiar with how the magazine staff-writers did their work, so he was given simply a roving commission. Miss Tarbell suggested that it might be worth while to have an

MISS IDA M. TARBELL

MISS VIOLA ROSEBORO'

article on certain admirable aspects of the city government of Cleveland. So Mr. Steffens went out there, with no definite idea in his mind. He went as far as Kansas City, Missouri, and in the office of the *Star*, a newspaper singularly well conducted by an editor and staff of unusual quality, he learned of the extraordinary work of Folk in St. Louis. He went to St. Louis and on his own initiative prepared an article on the revelations brought out at the trials that Folk had carried on against grafters. This article did not, to my mind, fully cover the subject, so that I soon had him back for an additional article. We published two articles on St. Louis.

Meantime I had learned of unbelievable conditions in Minneapolis, and I sent Mr. Steffens there. The situation in Minneapolis was so appalling, and the act of the citizens in electing Mayor Ames under the circumstances of that election so incomprehensible, that I entitled the article "The Shame of Minneapolis." The second article on St. Louis was entitled "The Shamelessness of St. Louis." Mr. Steffens' articles dealt in large part with material that had been brought out in the courts or by Grand Juries, and were instrumental in the first awakening of the American people to municipal administration.

After the Minneapolis article had shown the ap-

palling situation in that city, the Boston *Transcript*
stated that this sort of city government had really
nothing to do with the American people, who were
a highly moral and industrious people. It occurred
to me that if people could live as safely and upright
under laws that were made and administered by
crooks and incompetents, under a city government
like that of St. Louis, here was an anomaly in
civilization.

That thought led me to gather together from different sources statistics showing the comparative
number of murders, and the comparative amount of
fire and the comparative number of accidents in-
volving the loss of life. This investigation showed
that between 1881 and 1895 murder in the United
States had increased six times as rapidly as the
population—and that murder in the United States
was from ten to thirty times as much per million
inhabitants as in the countries of northwestern
Europe; that fire losses, burglaries, loss of life and
injury by accidents on railroads, in coal mines, fac-
tories, and so on, showed a similar condition, prov-
ing that government by dishonest and incompetent
men does not result in the protection of life and property. The results of this investigation I published
in December, 1904, during the publication of the
St. Louis articles and Miss Tarbell's articles. The

realization of the fact that life and property in the United States were less secure than in other countries, led me to go on making such studies as in time would arouse public opinion. Mr. Steffens' work dealing with the corruption of State and City politics was a feature of the magazine for three or four years.

These articles elicited an immediate response from the press, and undoubtedly had a strong influence upon the public mind. They were carefully and thoroughly worked out, and were, in so far as things made with human instruments can be, accurate. In fact, they were the first accurate studies of this nature that had then appeared in a magazine in America. To secure this accuracy, to make such studies of value, I had to invent a new method in magazine journalism.

The fundamental weakness of modern journalism, it seemed to me, was that the highly specialized activities of modern civilization were very generally reported by men uninformed in the subjects upon which they wrote. The one exception to this was the London *Times*, under Mr. Delane's management. Mr. Delane employed a staff of experts to report for him upon all subjects requiring special knowledge. He might employ the services of this or that expert only once in two years; but when a new discovery was made in science, or a new question arose in economics, he had at hand the man who could say all that was known on the subject.

The fault of this system, for my purpose, was that what the experts had to say was very seldom interesting to read. Men like Darwin and Tyndall and Huxley, who were at once great scientists and excellent writers, were few. I first began to read the works of Professor Tyndall when I was in college, and had always considered them models of interesting and comprehensible scientific writing. Later I knew both Huxley and Tyndall, and visited Tyndall at his beautiful place at Haslemere, and also at his Alpine home at Belalp. When I first began to have scientific articles reported for the magazine, I used to urge my writers to try to follow something like Tyndall's clear manner of presentation.

When I began to feel the necessity to handle economic questions in the magazine, the same difficulty confronted me. Most of our journalists were not accustomed to going into a question very thoroughly, and the trained students of the subject either could not write clearly, or they were warped by some special prejudice and devoted to some particular aspect of the subject. I decided, therefore, to pay my writers for their study rather than for the amount of copy they turned out—to put the writer on such a salary as would relieve him of all financial worry and let him master a subject to such a degree that he could write upon it, if not with the authority of the specialist, at least with such accuracy as could inform the public and meet with the corroboration of experts.

The articles produced under this system were generally called "*McClure* articles," and they were from the first recognized as authoritative. The preparation of each of these articles entailed, on the writer's part, the accumulation of knowledge and material enough to make a book. The preparation of the fifteen articles which made the Standard Oil series took Miss Tarbell five years. The articles were produced at the rate of about three a year, and cost the magazine about four thousand dollars each. Mr. Steffens averaged about four articles a year, and each article cost us about two thousand dollars. It was my experience that such articles as gave *McClure's Magazine* its peculiar standing can not be produced by a less expensive method. Of course, subjects that will repay the editor for so expensive a method of presentation are few and important.

Before Mr. Steffens joined the staff of *McClure's,* we had already engaged as a staff writer Mr. Ray Stannard Baker. While Mr. Baker was working on the Chicago *Daily News,* we had bought several articles and stories from him, and we found he had the qualities we wanted in our staff writers. It so happened that the January, 1903, number of *McClure's* which contained the third article of Miss Tarbell's Standard Oil series, also contained Mr. Steffens' Minneapolis article, and Mr. Baker's article on the anthracite coal strike of 1902.

Thus the origin of what was later called the "muck-raking" movement was accidental. It came from no formulated plan to attack existing institutions, but was the result of merely taking up in the magazine some of the problems that were beginning to interest the people a little before the newspapers and the other magazines took them up.

Miss Viola Roseboro' joined the staff of *McClure's* as manuscript reader soon after the magazine was started. At one time we had a prize contest for short stories, and so great a number of stories came in that I engaged Miss Roseboro', whom I knew well, to help me read them. This led to a permanent connection. Miss Roseboro' was of great service to the magazine in discovering promising material by unknown writers. She had a singularly open mind toward the manuscript bag, a natural attitude toward stories which is rare in professional readers, who, like everybody else, in time become the victims of their own tastes and their own successes, and are therefore always hunting for the thing they themselves like best, instead of for the thing that new writers are writing best. Miss Roseboro' seized upon the early stories of O. Henry, Jack London, Rex Beach, Myra Kelley, and the "Emmy Lou" stories when their writers were unknown, with as much sureness and conviction as if she had known what the end was to be in each case, and exactly how popular each of these writers was to become.

People often ask me how I got ideas for the magazine. An editor, of course, gets ideas from his interest in what is going on in the world; *being interested* is a large part of an editor's vocational equipment. Sometimes ideas came about things that were close at hand and easy to procure; sometimes an idea led me a long chase, as in the case of Miss Stone.

In the autumn of 1901 the newspapers were full of the capture of Miss Stone, an American missionary in Macedonia, by Bulgarian brigands in the Balkans. The newspaper campaign to raise money to ransom Miss Stone, and the widespread excitement concerning her fate, led the brigands—who were really revolutionists trying to raise money to buy arms to fight the Turks—to think they had captured an American citizen of such importance that they could ask any ransom they chose. They demanded $100,000, and, when this was refused, negotiations ceased, and Miss Stone and her companion, Mme. Tsilka, were unheard of by the world for months. I was in Switzerland with Mrs. McClure when rumors began to reach us that Miss Stone was still alive.

I went to Salonica, when I found that Mr. House, the head missionary there, and Mr. Tsilka, were about to go to Serres, on the Southern slope of the Rhodope Mountains, among which mountains Miss Stone and Madame Tsilka were supposed to be concealed. I accompanied them to Serres, and we waited there for about three weeks for news of the captives.

Mr. House and Mr. Tsilka knew what the Turks did not know—that the American mission at Bansko had delivered ransom money to the brigands, and that Miss Stone and Mme. Tsilka might be brought to Serres at any time. The American missionaries at Bansko had been closely watched by the Turkish soldiers, who knew that the missionaries had money for ransom. Their hope was to catch the missionaries treating with the brigands, open fire on them as traitors to the Turkish government, and seize the gold intended for the brigands. The Americans had in their saddle-bags in gold £14,000 Turk, an amount equal to $70,000, which had been raised in this country by popular subscription. The problem was to deliver this gold to the brigands without being swooped down upon by the Turkish soldiers. The Turkish soldiers, who surrounded the mission at Bansko under the pretext of guarding it, were really there to see that no gold went from the mission to the Bulgarian brigand-revolutionists. Every time the missionaries went out on horseback, their saddle-bags were weighed when they went forth and when they returned.

But, in spite of these extraordinary difficulties—right under the nose of the Turks—the Americans took three separate journeys, each carrying each time all he could of gold, and delivered the gold to the brigands. As they removed the gold from their saddle-bags they put in little leaden images of the exact weight of the gold removed, so that the bags always weighed the same.

When the missionaries at Bansko made their final payment of gold to the brigands, the brigands had agreed to deliver Miss Stone and her companion sound and safe at Serres, as soon as they could do so without running the risk of being attacked by other bands of brigands who were hoping to recapture Miss Stone and get another ransom. All this Mr. House and Mr. Tsilka knew. During the three

weeks that we spent in the little hotel at Serres we
expected the captives hourly. At last, however, we
grew impatient and concluded (which was indeed
the case) that the brigands were so closely watched
that they could not produce Miss Stone without
danger of her falling into the hands of other brigands,
or of the Turkish soldiers, where she would have
been infinitely worse off than with them. We never
suspected the Bulgarian brigands of bad faith,
for brigandage is one profession in which the
prosperity of a man's business absolutely depends
upon his scrupulously keeping his word. We decided
that the brigands were in such a predicament that
they could do nothing for the present, and we went
back to Constantinople to await further news.

After waiting some time, I decided to leave Turkey and return to Europe; so on a Saturday I got
my passport for Vienna. Sunday I went to bid Mr.
Leishman, the American minister, good-bye, and he
said: "Mr. McClure, if I were you I would not go
now; I think I would go to Serres. Word has been
received from Miss Stone, and she will arrive in
Serres Tuesday morning."

I went back to Serres, and met Miss Stone on the
afternoon of her arrival at Salonika. She came by
train, and I was the first person to board the train
after it pulled in at Salonika. After a short talk

with her, I arranged to get her account of her experience for *McClure's Magazine*. Madame Tsilka's baby, born after their capture, was then six months old, and had never slept under a roof. The two women had been well treated, but had gone through terrible hardships. Before Madame Tsilka's baby was born, the brigands had decided that they would kill it, because it would be so much in their way. The very night the baby was born, they decided to take a long and hazardous mountain journey, as the Turkish soldiers were pressing hard. Influenced by the pleadings of Miss Stone, however, they consented to wait until three days after the birth of the baby, when Mme. Tsilka, with her baby slung on her back, had to make with them this long and very rough journey on foot. The brigands were always fleeing from the Turks, and warned the women that if the baby cried they would have to kill it for safety.

I tell this story as an example of the adventures I sometimes had in getting material for the magazine. Of course, any one would have seen that Miss Stone's story would be interesting material for a magazine; but not infrequently the magazine's biggest successes were articles whose interest was generally doubted, even in my own office, until they had succeeded. My articles on Mme. Montessori's method of teaching young children were an example of that. Every one in the office said a pedagogical article could not possibly be interesting. When I was in London in the winter of 1910, Miss Mary L. Bisland, the London representative of *McClure's Magazine* who often secured splendid material for us, told me of the remarkable work that Mme. Montessori was doing at Rome in educating young children. Miss Bisland had got her information concerning Mme. Montessori's method from an old friend, Miss Josephine Tozier, who had spent some months in Rome, talking to Mme. Montessori and visiting her schools. Through Miss Bisland, I commissioned Miss Tozier to write an article on the Montessori method of teaching young children. Every important article that appears in *McClure's Magazine* is always submitted to persons who have special knowledge of the subject treated upon, for criticism and suggestion. When Miss Tozier's article was completed, it was carefully compared with Mme. Montessori's book—then untranslated—by the English critic, Mr. William Archer, who assured me that it adequately represented Mme. Montessori's theories. Before the article was published it was submitted to several authorities on kindergartening and pedagogy in the United States. These experts, I found, greatly differed in their estimates

MISS MARY L. BISLAND

DR. MARIA MONTESSORI

of Montessori's methods. Some of them were very antagonistic in their attitude, and declared that, because Mme. Montessori recognized and valued the work of great educators of the past, there was nothing new about her method.

Miss Tozier's article appeared in the May number of *McClure's*, 1911, and immediately letters of inquiry began to come into the office in such numbers that it was impossible to answer them all. Mme. Montessori, in Rome, found herself engulfed in such a correspondence as threatened to take all her time. It seemed as if people everywhere had been waiting for her message. In the winter of 1913 some eighty primary teachers from all over the world, from as far away as Australia, went to Rome to study the Montessori method.

Alexander Graham Bell, whose chief interest has always been in teaching and methods of teaching, although he is best known as the inventor of the telephone, told me that he considered the introduction of the Montessori system in the United States as the most important work that *McClure's Magazine* had ever done.

The method of dealing with public questions which distinguished *McClure's Magazine* was developed gradually. My desire to handle such questions in the magazine came about, I think, largely from my frequent trips abroad. I went to Europe three or four times every year, in the first place, because I got more ideas when I moved about and came in contact with interesting people, and, in the second, because my health was so uncertain that I had often to get away from my business. Physically, I was a worn-out man when I founded *McClure's Magazine*. I had never paid any attention to ways and means. I started to go to college with fifteen cents in my pocket; I went to Boston to get a job with $6 as my whole capital; I was penniless when I founded the syndicate. Working against odds of this kind, without money or influence, had told on my health, already overstrained in my boyhood by hard work and poor nutrition.

I had never thought of such a thing as economy of effort. When I had an idea, I pursued it; when I wanted anything, I went ahead and got it. My business associates, Albert Brady and Mr. Phillips, often counteracted the effects of my rashness in business, and saw to the ways and means of carrying out my plans. But I had squandered my strength more recklessly than I had squandered anything else, and nobody could help me to meet the overdraft I had made on my health.

When I was on the road, seeing editors, after my syndicate was well started, I used often to have to spend half the day in bed, in order to be strong enough to attend to business the other half. From 1890 on I was overcome more and more often by periods of complete nervous exhaustion, when I had to get out of my office and out of New York City, when I felt for my business the repulsion that a seasick man feels toward the food he most enjoys in health. Crossing the ocean seemed to relax this tension. New interests would take hold of me in London or Paris, and before I knew it I was picking up editorial ideas again. Good editorial work can only be done out of spontaneous personal interest; it can not be forced. To lose his enthusiasm is the worst thing that can happen to an editor—next to having been born without any. In Europe I always got a renewal of the power to be interested; and that, for me, was simply the power to edit an interesting magazine.

In my rapid trips back and forth from America to Europe, I noticed certain differences in the attitude of the people, here and abroad, regarding public service, and regarding the connection between business interests and government. I often noticed, for example, as compared with Berlin or Paris, the extraordinary filth that characterized New York City. I remember once, arriving in New York, getting into a street-car to go up from the boat, and saying to myself: "What dirty streets in this city; and what dirty cars in these dirty streets; and what dirty people in these dirty cars!"

When I was abroad I always had the New York and Chicago papers sent to me. The front page usually announced some horrible crime or accident or disaster. There was a savage note in the news as compared with European news. It was not that the foreign press was less diligent in reporting crimes and disasters, but that there were fewer to report. In London there is an obscure murder about once in three weeks; in New York City and in Chicago murders occur several times a week the year round. There are more bombs thrown with criminal intent in New York City than in all the rest of the world. There are more fires in New York City than in all the great European cities added together. There are more people burned alive in New York City every year than in all the great European capitals. Naturally, the newspapers read differently.

I was disappointed in the effects of Mr. Steffens' paper on the corrupt government of most of our large cities. It did not seem to me that the people were roused as they ought to be by the revelation that they were governed by the lowest classes in the community—often by criminals. In treating the subject Mr. Steffens had confined himself to the money waste and to the wretchedly poor public service resulting from this kind of municipal government. There was a darker side, which concerned the increase of crime and lawlessness, the traffic in vice, and the calculated debasing of men and women. I thought, if the people were informed about this, it would make a stronger appeal than financial waste to their moral sense, especially to that of the women, everywhere.

In the winter of 1906–1907 the Chicago papers were filled day by day with news that really revealed Chicago as a semi-barbarous country in which life and property were unsafe to an extraordinary degree. This daily crop of news would be duly accented by reports of horrible crimes. I had a selection made from these papers which gave a criminal record of Chicago for the winter and revealed an appalling situation. Now, it is a fact which I have observed that people will become accustomed to almost any environment. I remember, when I was in Turkey, where occasionally a village would be devastated, the children killed, the women tortured, that people in an adjacent village, who might be the victims any time, went about their work quite calmly and indifferently, so

that it is not suprising that this daily grist of news
of the Chicago crimes was accepted by the citizens
as a matter of course. They grew accustomed to
the fact that it was dangerous to traverse almost any
street after dark. From the material I had gathered
I made a selection sufficient to make a magazine
article, and sent Mr. George Kibbe Turner to
Chicago to write an introduction to this article,
which was made up solely of news or editorial
extracts from the Chicago papers. This resulted in
an article by Mr. Turner on Chicago that was the
beginning of a discussion on the degrading influences
in government connected with the exploitation of
women, and led to activities that subsequently
produced the Vice Commission Report on Chicago,
a document that goes far beyond any statements
made by Mr. Turner in his Chicago article. This
article attracted considerable attention in Chicago
and elsewhere, and in the next issue of the magazine,
May, 1907, I published an article made up from
excerpts from the Chicago newspapers entitled
"Chicago As Seen by Herself." Soon after this
Mr. Kennan's articles on San Francisco revealed the
same union between the political machines, the
actual government, and the exploitation of women.
An investigation made by us in different parts of the
country led us to make a study of the situation in

New York City on the same lines. The effect of these studies on the public mind was much more marked than of the studies which dealt solely with financial corruption.

In 1906 I began to notice references to the so-called commission form of government, and when Mr. Turner joined my staff he suggested that he prepare an article on the commission form of government as developed in Galveston, Texas. These articles appeared in October, 1906. At once I realized that here was found the basic remedy for the extraordinary inefficiency and misgovernment in American cities, and the magazine supported this method of reforming the city government. Mr. Steffens' articles, in dealing with municipal corruption, were generally expressed in terms of financial waste. But in all our investigations, and in fact in the general published reports in the newspapers, we found that these corrupt governments were kept in power largely by the votes of the most corrupt elements of the population—by the crooks, the criminals, saloonkeepers, gamblers, pool-room keepers, and so on; that in many instances the so-called political machine drew its power to deliver votes from this class. Mr. Steffens had shown how men, to secure important street franchises or contracts, had contributed money to support the corrupt governments. The new work of the magazine was to show how, by the organization of the most corrupt and debased people in a community, the political machine was able to turn over the funds. Corrupt city government, as we understand it in American States, benefits all classes who wish to get advantage, either by breaking the laws or by having bad laws made; it benefits the capitalist, who can thereby get important franchises; it benefits the saloonkeeper who can keep his saloon open nights and Sundays; it benefits all those who want money that they do not work for.

It seemed to me that one of the most important fields of inquiry would be to study different populations under different governments, and, making allowances for the fixed conditions as to territory, climate, soil, etc., find out which people, on the whole, were best governed and which governments were the most successful as governments. I was desirous of finding out why, in American cities as distinguished from American States, the debasing and debased part of the population should have a predominating influence in nominating and electing officials. There was nothing in history that would explain this difference, and it was only by a study of our commission form of government, and a study of the methods organizing governments in England and Germany, that I came to understand the basic causes for the inefficiency and corruption of governments in American cities, and the only way to secure good government.

There are two basic causes for the failure of governments in America. One may be briefly called the theory of Rousseau, which claims that a way to secure good government is to have all the elected officials elected directly by the people, and that these officials should be for a very short term of office, not more than a year. It failed because the conditions of employment were so disagreeable that the best men would not take office, the length of employment so brief that no one could afford to qualify for the office or could expect to be qualified by experience. Further, the very length of the tickets, together with the huge and cumbersome machinery of nominations, brought about a condition that actually put the nominations into the hands of a small group of men, so that the actual voting people had almost no choice in regard to a nomination. The other cause of failure of government in America was based upon the theory that first became prominent in the writings of Montesquieu, in which the idea was set forth that the people can have freedom under government only if the government is organized so that different institutions of government will be a check each upon the other. This developed, in the American Constitution, to a government of divided powers, a government of checks and balances, where the executive and the judiciary and the legislative each was a check upon the others. This principle was incorporated in the State governments and the city governments. It was proved, wherever tried—in the South American republics and the United States—to be a most disastrous principle in governments.

I found, by studying different forms of government, that where crime was small in amount, where there were good laws for the protection of workingmen, where there were good laws which resulted in very small fire losses, that there the governments were identical and simple; namely, the people elected only a board of directors. Extraordinarily well governed German cities elect only a board of directors and no other kind of officials, and this board of directors employs the Mayor and other city officials. This method is identical with the so-called commission form of government in America. This form of government is purely and solely representative. Being simple and natural, it involves a very simple electoral system. In a German city there are no preëlection activities recognized by law—no conventions, no primary elections, no method of legally getting an official's name on a ticket. When an election occurs, the very first act of a German citizen is to go to the polls and vote for any man who is eligible. It sometimes happens that no one has a majority; within eight days the two highest names are voted for, and the one that has the majority becomes a councilor. The ticket of a German citizen, is therefore, one name long—it may be his own creation or that of a group of friends. This happens once in six years, and constitutes the entire electoral activity of a citizen of a German city, who secures an amount of self-rule that we can not conceive of in America. This simplicity of government renders unnecessary the somewhat dangerous organs of government known as the Initiative, the Referendum, and the Recall.

The commission form of government is the universal form where efficiency is secured, and it is the form adopted by corporations all over the world; it is the form of all leading governments of leading countries—England, Germany, Demark, Switzerland, Holland—Northwestern Europe; it is the universal form by which groups of men, organized to carry out a common purpose, whether members of a church, owners of a bank or railroad, or members of a labor union—proceed to carry out their purpose.

The average American citizen often apologizes for his indifference to public questions by saying that under a loose and careless government the individual has more freedom than under a well organized government; that the United States would do ill to pattern after any European form of government, however efficient; and that graft is the price we pay for democracy. Yet the only two foreign countries in which graft is as prevalent as it is here are Spain and Russia, countries where the individual is badly off. I once spent some time in Seville, inquring into the municipal system, and found a more unblushing state of things than has ever existed in any American city. The Mayor of Seville, I found, always got rich during his term of office. His methods were very simple. One of them was to condemn the paving of a certain street, order the paving removed, pave another street with the same material, and collect from the city for it. Most of his devices were as obvious as this one. The people made no objection, because they were used to it. In St. Petersburg I found instances where battleships had been officially designed, built, armored, manned, money drawn therefor, and the ships were entirely a myth—not a nail had ever been driven. Every one knows that, in the war with Japan, Russia was defeated by graft. She could have contracted for the Siberian Railway with a reliable English firm for $250,000,000. Built by Russia herself, with all the graft, the Siberian railway cost $500,000,000, and was so poor as to be almost useless under the urgent demands of war.

When I came to this country, an immigrant boy, in 1866, I believed that the government of the United States was the flower of all the ages—that nothing could possibly corrupt it. It seemed the one of all human institutions that could not come to harm. This feeling was general, at home and abroad. The nation had, during the Civil War, risen to moral heights which it has never since attained. The war itself resulted in the opening of easy avenues of corruption. During the struggle, and for years before, everything else had been neglected for the one great question of slavery. People felt that if this were righted, nothing could be wrong. The great resources of the continent were rapidly opening up, with no provision being made to control them, or to control the few able men who were bound to seize and utilize these unparalleled resources for their own ends. After the war came the evils of carpet-bag government in the South, and the corruption attending the pension

266

system. The American people went on believing that they were still what they once had been, but they were not.

As a foreign-born citizen of this country, I would like to do my part to help to bring about the realization of the very noble American Ideal, which, when I was a boy, was universally believed in, here and in Europe. I believe that the dishonest administration of public affairs in our cities has come about largely through carelessness, and that the remedy is as simple, as easily understood, and as possible of attainment, as the remedy for typhoid fever. The remedy is no dangerous experiment. It was adopted in Germany in the latter part of the last century. As a matter of self-protection it was adopted by Great Britain in the first third of the last century, and it lifted the nation out of as corrupt conditions of government as had ever existed. It was adopted by Galveston, after the great flood of 1901, to enable that city to continue its existence as a city. This very simple remedy is the establishment, in every municipality, of what, in a railroad, is called a board of directors, in a German city is called the Council, and in an American city is called the commission form of government.

THE END

Books by Willa Cather Published by
the University of Nebraska Press

Alexander's Bridge

April Twilights, Revised Edition
ed. with an intro. by Bernice Slote

The Autobiography of S. S. McClure

The Kingdom of Art: Willa Cather's First Principles and
Critical Statements, 1893–1896
*selected and ed. with two essays and a commentary
by Bernice Slote*

My Ántonia
ed. by Charles Mignon and Kari Ronning

A Lost Lady
*ed. by Charles W. Mignon, Frederick M. Link, and
Kari A. Ronning*

Not Under Forty

O Pioneers!
*ed. by Susan J. Rosowski and Charles W. Mignon with
Kathleen Danker*

The Troll Garden: A Definitive Edition
ed. by James Woodress

Uncle Valentine and Other Stories: Willa Cather's
Uncollected Short Fiction
ed. with an intro. by Bernice Slote

Willa Cather in Europe: Her Own Story of the
First Journey

Willa Cather in Person: Interviews, Speeches, and Letters
ed. by L. Brent Bohlke

Willa Cather on Writing: Critical Studies on
Writing as an Art

Willa Cather's Collected Short Fiction, 1892–1912
*Revised Edition ed. by Virginia Faulkner with intro. by
Mildred R. Bennett*